What others are saying

If You Give a Girl a Giant...

Looking for a book that will help you to become all God wants you to be? In *If You Give a Girl a Giant* Karen Porter skillfully gives us the weapons we need to fight off our personal giants. This book is filled with intriguing stories of women like you who applied God's truth to their challenges, changed their thinking, and celebrated their victories. Read it on your own, or gather a group of friends together and discuss the content together. I love this book!

Carol Kent, Speaker and Author
He Holds My Hand (Tyndale)

My heart and faith was strengthened by Karen Porter when she shared that there is no giant, no lie, no adversary that the name of the Lord cannot overcome. From a very familiar story comes a new and profound perspective that God fights for us. No bullies allowed any longer in my life! Karen's wit, transparency, and obvious knowledge of the Word of God makes her one of my favorite writers and speakers of all time.

Vicki Heath, Author, Speaker,
National Director, First Place for Health

Everyone who is facing a giant in their life needs this book. Karen Porter brings insight and encouragement for your journey — reminding all of us that God is bigger than our battles. Her fresh approach and real-life stories communicate God's truth in a fun and relevant way. Get this book today and find God's victory for you.

Andrea Booth, Author, Women's Ministry Leader.
Andrea and her husband Garrett Booth pastor Grace
Church, Houston

Fighting our giants is hard, but Karen has authentically walked alongside us and taught us to stay in the fight. She weaves a story of courage and possibility through every chapter of hope. I can honestly say I'm excited to stand and fight. She's given us the weapons to know how.

Gari Meacham
Author of *Spirit Hunger, Watershed Moments,* and *Be Free.*
President and Co-founder of The Vine Uganda

With a measure of success, many writers can come up with self-help material that might connect with the intellect. But Karen reaches far deeper than the intellect; she reaches the heart. God has periodically allowed her to experience life in the trenches. And whatever God allowed her to experience was never without purpose. Because she shares from the depths of her heart, she reaches the hearts of her readers.

Paul Gauntt, Author,
Pastor, First Baptist Church, Palmer, Texas

Karen Porter has outdone herself on her newest book. I love everything Karen has written but this book is sure to hit a nerve with most of us because we know all too well the giants of discouragement, defeat, fear and self. I especially like that this book will be easy to teach in a group setting of four to six weeks. The insights about Goliath and his brothers were new to me and most likely will be to the reader as well.

Carole Lewis
First Place 4 Health Director Emeritus
Author, *Live Life, Right Here, Right Now*

If You Give a Girl a Giant...

If You Give a Girl a Giant...

Fighting for Your Life

Karen Porter

Bold Vision Books
PO Box 2011
Friendswood, Texas 77549

Dedication

To Cherry, daughter, wife,
mom,
extraordinary woman of God,
and
giant slayer.

You are my encourager
and you have pushed me to
excellence. Thank you.

Thanks for the smiles, fun, and
joy you bring into my life.

Table of Contents

A Note from the Author

There are some surprises in a few obscure verses in 2 Samuel chapter 21. Four giants and four mighty warriors are named. The surprise is in the meanings of their names. Each giant is familiar to your life, and each warrior represents the weapon God has provided.

I want you to discover these secrets so you can slay giants.

Make no mistake, the giants want to destroy you and me. To confuse, condemn, and cause us to fail. If they can't destroy, they want to distract us from God's path. Each giant seems not so tall until we meet it face to face. But these sassy giants strut and sting our souls. Too often each giant is more insidious than the one before, eager to get us down. They try new strategies if the previous ones didn't work. The giants keep coming around.

We are not equipped to fight the battle. But God gives us the weapons to outsmart each giant who dares to raise its ugly head. Unless we have God's weapons, we will never reach the potential He has planned for us.

This book is a spiritual book. You may wish to tackle your giants with plans, charts, budgets, and to-do lists but the battle is spiritual.

In these pages, you will learn how to fight for your life, get rid of a victim mentality and let God lift your heavy burdens. There is a place for you to reflect and respond in the "What's a Girl to Do" sections.

Don't fight the giants alone.

Join me. With His help, we will fight for our lives.

Karen

Prologue

srael's Elah Valley stretched as far as I could see. On each side, a rocky ridge rose and then flattened like an ocean after a wave.

A rowdy group from our tour experimented with the homemade sling our guide had provided. They gathered smooth stones from the dry streambed to drop into the sling's leather pouch and then whirled the strap overhead to launch the pebble as far as they could. Some pebbles fell. Some wobbled. Some catapulted directly to their targets.

I took in the view, pondering the place. It seemed like a theater stage set, ready for the director's command, "Action!" And then I remembered where I was. The valley looked like a stage because it *was* a stage. For in this valley thousands of years ago, an epic battle raged.

In that battle, on one of those ridges camped an army so fierce their name became synonymous with barbarian warrior.[1] On the other ridge stood the army of Almighty God.

The narrow valley permitted each army to watch the other, yet the camps on the parallel peaks stood distant enough to separate the soldiers—as long as no one moved.

The tension intensified each day. Which band of mighty men would dare to take a position in the valley? Two monumental armies at an impasse.

With the battle line drawn through the middle of the valley, the two armies stalemated on the parallel ridges. Then out of the barbaric ranks, a man stepped forward; some say he was nine-feet tall and wore 200 pounds of armor. The willowy grass flattened with each step. I picture him with ragged hair and a scraggly beard framing his face. He taunted, "I am the Philistine champion!"

On the Israeli ridge, the fearful soldiers crouched low behind their tents. And King Saul, the tallest man in camp, shrank behind the others.

Goliath, the ultimate bully, laughed, spitting words like, "Send out your best fighter. We'll settle the war one-on-one—with a single fight."

In the village of Bethlehem, a small town a few miles away, an old man named Jesse asked his youngest son, who was too young to be in the military, to take supplies to his brothers.

When young David reached the valley, he heard the taunting screams from Goliath and witnessed the Israeli army cowering. David may have been naïve about warfare, but he wasn't afraid.

David had seen God in action before. As the youngest son, David held the lowly job of shepherd for his father's sheep. He spent weeks and months in the desert with the flocks, an inconsequential job. But while living in the desert, David observed the wonders of creation and became acquainted with the Creator—Almighty God. When a bear and a lion attacked the sheep, God gave David the strength to kill both. Through God rescuing him from these wild animals and the communion he experienced with God on the hillside, David became intimately acquainted with the power of the God of the universe. David knew first-hand how God delivers from danger.

When David faced Goliath the giant, David believed God would show His power again. So, in front of two great armies, a young boy would fight a nine-foot warrior. David paused a moment to grab a few smooth round stones from the brook.

Into the Elah valley, David ran toward Goliath answering Goliath's taunt with truth. David shouted, "I come to you in the name of the LORD of Heaven's Armies—the God of the armies of Israel, whom you have defied."

David put a stone in his slingshot, whirled it overhead, and hit his mark—the forehead of Goliath. When the giant fell, the rest of the Philistines ran away.

Israel's formerly-less-than-courageous army found new audacity and chased the now-on-the-run barbarian warriors.

Applause. Roll the credits. We love this happy ending.

David becomes King. All is well.

No one would remember
David if he had killed a gnat.

Introduction

Each person faces Goliath. We are doomed because we are born with a sin nature. We are sinners. "For everyone has sinned; we all fall short of God's glorious standard" (Romans 3:23).

No exceptions—everyone. The path of sin leads to death. The Bible describes it as payment. "For the wages of sin is death" (Romans 6:23a). We deserve death.

But Jesus died. For me. For you. And His death—because He was perfect—pays the debt we owe. He is the alternative who offers us freedom from the penalty. "The free gift of God is eternal life through Christ Jesus our Lord" (Romans 6:23b).

Christ forfeited his throne in heaven to live as a human here on earth. He endured the pain and misery of torture and death by hanging on the cross and dying because He loves you.

Death was not the end. On the third day after lying dead in the tomb, He arose from the dead. His resurrection offers life to us.

Bible teacher, Billy Graham, explained the death and resurrection, "Both Jesus' death on the cross and His resurrection from the dead are equally important; they cannot be separated from each other. Without Jesus' death, we have no hope of God's forgiveness; and without Jesus' resurrection, we have no hope of eternal life. Like the two wings of an airplane, both are essential."[2]

Jesus offers the gift that slays the giant of sin—our Goliath. Our acceptance of His gift defeats Goliath forever. How do we accept the gift?

Paul answers this question, "If you openly declare that Jesus is Lord and believe in your heart that God raised him from the dead, you will be saved" (Romans 10:9).

Salvation is that simple. Trust—believe—in your heart. Declare—confess—with your mouth. Then your life is forever changed because Jesus changes you. He will give new desires, new thoughts, new hopes and dreams—and victory over Goliath.

Have you felt sorry for your sin? Do you believe that Jesus took your place in eternal death? When you say, "Yes" to Him, accepting His gift of life, you strike the fatal blow to Goliath.

When you and I allow Jesus to enter our hearts—and our lives—victory over death both here on earth and after we die is complete. We will never face Goliath again. Jesus' death and resurrection is enough to complete the deal and save us for eternity. But we aren't living in our eternal home yet. We must live here on earth, and there are more battles, and we will meet many more giants. The giants keep coming. Goliath lost the big battle, but giants want to disrupt and destroy any influence you might have on others. Giants lurk around you waiting for the moment when they can step in and crush you.

I'd be Okay if it Weren't for the Giants in my Backyard

I haven't seen any nine-foot beasts loitering in my back yard lately, but I know about giants who mock while I cringe in discouragement, defeat, and fear. You know them, too.

I made a bills-due list compared to expected income. I heard the giant laugh, "You'll never catch up. Why don't you give up?"

When once again I snapped impatiently at my beloved mother, the giant roared, "How could you? After all she's done for you?"

When my boss failed to invite me to a meeting, the giant mocked, "You don't matter."

When my girlfriend forgot my birthday, the taunting giant

muttered, "No one cares." And when I forgot her birthday, the giant snarled, "You are so selfish."

At each turn, the giants spew venom, "You are worthless. You failed again. I'm bigger than you. Your God isn't real." I become like those Israelite soldiers shaking in my sandals behind the tent, hoping no one will see that I am a fraud and that I don't want to fight.

Maybe your giant is your job—that success you fought to reach. The hours at graduate school, the résumés you sent out, and the headhunter's fees you paid. Finally, you landed the dream job only to discover that the work isn't interesting—much less glamorous. You feel used. Irrelevant. You wonder if you'll ever make it to the inside group of top-level execs.

Perhaps you selected the teacher route. You love teaching but now you aren't sure whether it's the kids or the parents who care less about education. The monotonous paperwork and binding restrictions are so severe that you rarely see one of those magical moments when a child's eyes light up with understanding.

Maybe you decided on the professional arena or you learned a craft only to feel stuck and bound as you struggle to follow the regulations and expectations.

What if you became a doctor. Hard work combined with long hours of on-the-job training only to feel bullied by an insurance bureaucracy and hospital administrators. As you manage indescribably terrible illnesses, you feel pushed to double-book every appointment slot to see more patients, but you haven't reaped the money or prestige that tantalized during those early days of medical school. The stress is endless and you yearn to experience that moment when a patient is cured.

Suppose you elected the sales route. You're a natural. You can convince anyone to buy what he or she doesn't even need. You expected to saturate your territory and reap those sweet bonus checks, but the quotas are set too high, the price structure prevents you from making the deals, and your competitors undercut every gain.

Maybe your company sold out to a huge conglomerate. Once you were a valued employee on a first name basis with the owner; now you're a computer number at headquarters two thousand miles away. Your hours get extended every week. The pressure builds. You are not sure you can take much more.

What if your giant is a mountain of laundry and endless chores? You chose to be a stay-at-home mom, but you feel like a slave.

When you awoke this morning, achy stiffness reminded that you are over fifty and your dreams are vaporized by reality. You wonder, "Is it too late?"

You long for another child but your husband says, "No way." The subject grows like a giant wall between the two of you.

You've spent thousands to cure infertility only to face disappointment when the newest treatment failed—again.

You dreamed you might do something great for God; even telling Him you'd go to the mission field when you were a teen, but now you have a family, a house, and a job.

You feel under-utilized at work, at home, and most disappointingly, at church too. Instead of important work, you are left with menial chores. Like David, you bring snacks while others are on the battlefield.

Something gnaws at you. *Why am I here? What is life about? Is this all there is?* You have a hole in your inner-most being that feels empty, dark, and cold. You long for something or someone to fill it. The glamour and bright lights lured but don't deliver. Giants loom as if living in your back yard.

Once while traveling to a small city, I climbed the six steps protruding from the side of a commuter plane—a runt replica next to the jets lined up on the tarmac. Inside, twelve rows crowded close to the narrow aisle. I settled by the window on row eleven, my small frame snug and comfortable on the padded chair.

A huge squared-shaped man pushed his way down the center of the plane, stopped at my row, and lowered himself into the tiny aisle seat next to me. I was completely dwarfed. He had total control of the leg room, the head room, the arm rest, and the air we breathed. *Is this how David felt when he stepped out on the valley floor?*

Our giants show up when we are most comfortable. We sit like a grownup in our assigned seat with our seat belts fastened. Then a giant takes his place next to us, and we are helpless. We dance with elephants with no space to maneuver.

Why Did David Pick up 5 Stones?

When we hear about David and Goliath, we are amazed to see the miracle and the young boy's victory, but one question always gnaws at me. Why did David reach into that brook and pick up 5 stones? He only needed one.

I believe David picked up the other four stones because he thought that he might have to fight Goliath's four brothers.

Goliath was the son of a man named Rapha, a descendant of Anak. Rapha fathered at least five sons—each one fiercer than the other.

David didn't fight the brothers that first day because the Philistines ran away after Goliath was killed. And though Israel chased after them, they didn't conquer the barbarians completely. The battles with the Philistines continued for years. David would face them later.

Giants Are Like That

David's reign as King of Israel continued for forty years. He won battles, defeating armies and regimes throughout the land. He built cities and palaces. His success was heralded around the world. He was a man after God's heart who wrote songs and psalms. But peace never came because rogue nations and bully warriors attacked, trying to take down the great king and nation. Each spring, when the weather cooperated, there would be new battles. (See 2 Samuel 11:1; 1 Chronicles 20:4). As David grew older, he was unable to fight with the same vigor as when he was young. His generals noticed.

"Once again the Philistines were at war with Israel. And when David and his men were in the thick of battle, David became weak and exhausted. Then David's men declared, 'You are not going out to battle with us again! Why risk snuffing out the light of Israel?'" (2 Samuel 21:15, 17b).

Wouldn't you know, that was the night one of Goliath's brothers came into David's camp seeking revenge. The giant's name was Ishbi-Benob.

Giant 1

Discouragement

Chapter 1
The Giant

"Ishbi-Benob was a descendant of the giants;
his bronze spearhead weighed more than seven
pounds, and he was armed with a new sword.
He had cornered David and was about to kill
him" (2 Samuel 21:16).

Imagine the vengefulness that had been simmering all these
years since Ishbi-Benob's brother Goliath had been slain by a
boy, of all people. David had not only killed Goliath, but had
also humiliated the family by taking the prized family sword.

"Then David ran over and pulled Goliath's
sword from its sheath. David used it to kill
him and cut off his head.... David took the
Philistine's head to Jerusalem, but he stored
the man's armor in his own tent"
(1 Samuel 17:51, 54).

Ishbi-Benob was a fierce fighter fueled by years of fury. This anger made him relentless in his attack on David and David's men.

The Hebrew name Ishbi-Benob means to sit down or tarry or make no progress. As he came into the camp, can't you hear him yelling, "Turn back; give up!"

Ishbi-Benob is the giant of discouragement.

The Giant of Discouragement

The giant of discouragement shows up when we least expect him. When we think we are doing okay, we can be blind-sided by pessimism or a feeling of gloom. It is far too easy for me to get discouraged. Someone doesn't smile at me, so I feel unloved. That someone might be experiencing a bad day or be distracted, but I figure if they didn't smile, it is my fault. I wonder what I did—and those inward thoughts lead me downhill to discouragement.

As I run my business or begin a creative venture, I seek to be successful. Sometimes my plans do not work out, so I feel stuck. Those feelings push me further, making me feel as if I have no talents or abilities—and then, discouragement settles in.

In the corporate world, there seems to be a new turf battle every week. Each hopeful manager vies for the next promotion. Or the company reorganizes. Or a new market challenges.

Physically, I've been on a 20-year perpetual diet. I do well and eat clean for weeks, but then one day I order pizza. The giant whispers, "*What's the point of dieting?*"

As a writer and speaker, I've seen the wheels of opportunity turn slowly, and I want to give up.

I plant a garden, and the weeds spring up.

The laundry piles grow.

It seems discouragement hits me no matter where I turn.

I saw a beautiful navy-blue quilt, decorated with an intricate design of candle-wicking stitches. Mesmerized, I ordered the kit to make one for myself. I had never tried to embroider a French knot before, and I'm not particularly handy at needlecraft. Within a few hours, I was discouraged. I rolled the fabric into a ball, tossing the whole thing into a trash can. *Why do I take on projects that don't match my skill set?*

Discouragement sets in and tries to take over—looming like a giant.

I was in the corporate world for many years and rose through the ranks to become one of the first women vice presidents in our male-dominated industry. I loved my job and all the perks that came with it. I loved managing the departments under me and working with the senior corporate management team to steer the company in the direction of success. I thrived on making decisions and deals. I reached a pinnacle that allowed me to travel around the world and meet heads of state. I committed the company to contracts worth millions of dollars with my signature. I admit the job was heady stuff. I developed a persona—my identity from the position and power. I became "Corporate Karen."

I loved this identity. I was aggressive and feisty. Every new customer was a challenge to me—especially if he wanted to talk to the "man" in charge. As the only woman executive, I relished these kinds of calls and was determined to conquer the caller like a personal Mt. Everest. The hard work paid off, too. Good promotions. Perks. Cars. Travel. Position—fame in my little world. I achieved a success few women reached at the time. Along the way, my boss believed in me, clients trusted me, and my family cheered me on. I had earned the privileges of success through hard work, and I happened to be in the right place at the right time to obtain a position in the inner circle of high-level corporate executives.

One morning, as I worked at my mahogany desk in my beautiful private office, the president of the company called me into his office, as he often did. I gathered the latest market reports and newest packaging designs because I knew he would want that information. When I entered his office, he held papers in his hands and without looking up said, "Sit down."

Then he looked up, "It grieves me to tell you this, but your job has been eliminated."

After thirty-three years, a half-dozen owners and managers, and working for this man—who had been my boss and colleague all these years and who once said I was his greatest friend in business—my illustrious career crashed with thirteen words.

No explanation. No fanfare.

"What did I do wrong?"

No answer.[3]

I hardly breathed as I cleared my desk.

When I got home to the beautiful house we'd built on some acreage in the rolling hills and thick forests north of town, I collapsed in my favorite chair, the one in the glamorous, fussily-designed office.

I cried. I pulled an afghan up over my ears and wailed. Every emotion from blaming myself to blaming everyone else blasted through me. Frightened for the future and wounded with rejection, something dark and sad—that I'm-no-longer-needed feeling—flooded over me.

Rejection.

Failure.

Disaster.

Then, I felt duped. All those years of hard work, making someone else rich.

Then I ranted—angry and outraged.

Then I felt like a failure.

I pounded my fist at their audacity.

I hammered myself for failing.

My battle was a roller coaster ride of emotions. Up with fury then down to the lowest depth of insignificance.

From, "How could they do this to *me*?"

To, "I must be worthless."

I agonized over what we would do financially—knowing we'd probably be forced to sell this new house that had become home to us.

Worries flooded my mind and crowded anger as I thought of finding a new job, moving to who knew where, and a thousand details like bills, upcoming events, and what to say to others. I hated losing the freedom that a large salary brings, but most of all, I grieved over the loss of my identity. Who was I now if I was no longer "Corporate Karen?"

The sorrow and anguish were tangible as discouragement dug its talons into me.

In *The Screwtape Letters,* C. S. Lewis crafts a clever tale of a senior tempter teaching a novice how to defeat a Christian. The master, Uncle Screwtape, teaches his young nephew, Wormwood, "In every department of life, it [discouragement] marks the transition from dreaming aspiration to laborious doing." Uncle Screwtape describes how God gave His children freedom to make decisions and thus potentially face disappointment. And he maliciously whispers to young Wormwood, "And there lies our opportunity."[4]

Discouragement is indeed an opportunity for the devil. Discouragement is a confusion for us believers. Because its causes can be so elusive, discouragement has been called the hardest emotion to explain. But even when we don't know its source, discouragement casts a blue cloud, bringing with it a chill and unmistakable pain.

Remember Joseph. He faced the giant of discouragement repeatedly. His story is detailed in the last chapters of the Bible book of Genesis. He lived in a dysfunctional family. His brothers were jealous. His father played favorites, preferring Joseph and Benjamin over the other sons because he liked the mother of Joseph and Benjamin most.

Sounds like the plot of a soap opera.

As a young fellow, Joseph aggravated the family situation by telling dreams of his brothers bowing to him. Then the brothers hated Joseph so much, they plotted to kill him, but at the last minute opted to sell him to slave traders instead. Joseph was taken from familiar fields and from his doting father to a big city where no one knew his name. He got a job serving a nobleman but that job ended when the wife attempted to seduce Joseph and lied about him when he didn't respond to her advances. Joseph was convicted without a trial and sent to prison.

When the Pharaoh's cupbearer and baker also landed in prison, Joseph was assigned to assist them. (See Genesis 40:4.) Imagine his disappointment and his anguish. Imprisoned for doing nothing wrong and a crime he did not commit. Now he was serving two servants.

Discouragement feels unfair and sad. Hope disappears when we are discouraged. Time moves slowly, and answers seem impossible. Joseph asked the cupbearer to remember him, to help get him out of prison when the cupbearer was released. But weeks, months, years later, Joseph still sat in prison. No relief and no release from prison. How sad and discouraged Joseph must have felt.

The giant of discouragement laughs in the background.

The great prophet Elijah loved and trusted God. Miracles surrounded his life. God sent ravens to feed him. God caused a widow's oil to overflow during drought and famine. Elijah called fire from heaven in front of a hostile crowd of false-god-worshipping people. He once outraced a horse on foot. Elijah faced Queen Jezebel with courage and power. Until she threatened him.

"When Ahab got home, he told Jezebel everything Elijah had done, including the way he had killed all the prophets of Baal. So, Jezebel sent this message to Elijah: 'May the gods strike me and even kill me if by this time tomorrow I have not killed you just as you killed them'" (1 Kings 19:1-2).

Perhaps experiencing the simple exhaustion that typically follows huge spiritual triumphs, discouragement took Elijah on a downward spiral into sadness and despair. He ran away to hide feeling like he could and, maybe should, die.

The giant of discouragement laughs in the background.

No matter how high the mountaintop experience, fatigue leaves us susceptible to discouragement. Maybe Elijah was discouraged because he expected the king and queen to turn to the Lord after the miraculous events on Mt. Carmel. Maybe he was overtired when he heard the murderous threats of Jezebel. It's clear he thought he was all alone.

"Elijah replied, 'I have zealously served
the LORD God Almighty. But the people of
Israel have broken their covenant with you, torn
down your altars, and killed every one of your
prophets. I am the only one left, and now they
are trying to kill me, too'" (1 Kings 19:10).

Whatever brought it on, the giant of discouragement was ready and waiting for Elijah, shouting words of rejection, dejection, guilt, and failure.

Perhaps the best description of discouragement is found in Psalm 102. We don't know the name of the psalmist but the Bible describes the author of the psalm as the prayer of a person overwhelmed with trouble. Maybe you will relate to the pain as you read the words of this Psalm.

"For my days vanish like smoke;
my bones burn like glowing embers.
My heart is blighted and withered like grass;
I forget to eat my food.
In my distress, I groan aloud
and am reduced to skin and bones.
I am like a desert owl,
like an owl among the ruins.
I lie awake; I have become
like a bird alone on a roof.
All day long my enemies taunt me;
those who rail against me use my name as a curse.

For I eat ashes as my food
and mingle my drink with tears
because of your great wrath,
for you have taken me up and thrown me aside.
My days are like the evening shadow;
I wither away like grass" (Psalm 102: 3-11 NIV).

We seldom have control over *when* the giant of discouragement steps into our space. He comes and goes at will, frequently at the times we have the fewest resources for fighting him. We hear him laughing in the background. Though we can't stop him from shouting his disheartening words, we can retrace our steps to recognize from where he slithered. We can counter his dismal, hopelessness with truth. We can lasso the pain of discouragement. We can push ourselves to think positively. We can learn to deal with the pain of discouragement, and we can push ourselves to think positively, but we'll never defeat the giant—alone.

Chapter 2
The Weapon

"But Abishai son of Zeruiah came to David's
rescue and killed the Philistine"
(2 Samuel 21:17).

When the giant named Ishbi-Benob charged into David's
camp, a mighty warrior named Abishai killed the giant. As
one of David's bravest mighty men, Abishai was dedicated to
David throughout David's life. He fled with David from the
murderous threats of King Saul into the Wilderness of Ziph.
He alone accompanied David into Saul's tent, and he defended
David and was the officer in charge in many battles—with the
Edomites, Syrians, Ammonites, and others. Abishai could run
like a gazelle. He was a chief of armies and once slew more than
300 men with his spear. "Abishai's best trait was his unswerving
loyalty to David."[5] He was steadfast no matter what the situation.
(See 1 Samuel 26; 2 Samuel 2, 3, 10, 16, 18, 19, 20.)

Abishai represents the faithfulness of God.

There is no better weapon against the giant of discouragement
than God's faithfulness.

God is trustworthy and dependable. We can count on Him. Throughout history, when humans fail, God faithfully shows up. God was faithful before, and He will be faithful again. He has never broken a promise, and He never will. He is faithful. Even if it feels as if He has failed you, perhaps due to a tragedy or other cruelty caused by humans, He is faithful—whether you can see it or not.

When people let me down by lying or failing to keep their promises. When a friend is not loyal. When organizations and companies betray. When we are careless and disappointed in ourselves. When someone ignores our pleas for help. When we are discontent with our lack of success. When our dreams collapse or our hopes take a nosedive. God is faithful.

As I sat in my home office on the day of my job loss, I felt overwhelmed by the giant of discouragement. Injustice and unfairness are not-so-good parts of this bent world we live in, and I felt wronged and wounded.

A battle raged within me. Members of the discouragement team duked it out in my home office. Fury vs. humiliation.

On one side of the fight was anger. *They can't do that to me!*

On the other side was shame. *If they did this to me, I must be worthless.*

I screamed, "I'll sue."

And then hung my head and wept, "I'll die."

My office featured large plate-glass windows on each wall revealing a view of the woods I adored. I battled my heartbreak and pain in the big chair until the shadows moved down the tree trunks and up the side of the house as twilight eclipsed the back lawn. I picked up my worn Bible and opened it to the Psalms hoping for some help from those ancient songs I habitually read every day. I mindlessly scanned the pages for a while and then stopped at a verse.

"You will not die..." (Psalm 118:17).

I laughed out loud. God's Word rescued me, reminding me that God is faithful in every situation—even when I think I might die.

You can count on Him, too. He is worthy of your trust. He dotes on you like a father adores his child. He feels what you feel. He weeps along with you. He will show you the path through discouragement.

No matter how your discouragement has beaten you down, God is faithful. And if you blame yourself for the discouragement, He is still faithful. Pope Francis said, "His faithfulness is stronger than our unfaithfulness."

The famous preacher, Charles Spurgeon said, "No sin of ours has ever made him unfaithful." The Apostle Paul wrote,

> ## "If we are unfaithful, he remains faithful, for he cannot deny who he is" (2 Timothy 2:13).

Discouragement happens when we try to make it alone, but we can't do it. Only His faithfulness is able to destroy the giant of discouragement.

We need Him.

Why does God allow us to get discouraged? It seems like a logical question. If He loves me and is faithful to me…why?

God not only dwells in us, He delights in us. He does not leave us drifting without purpose. He sees the great in our future. Even when we think we are doing well, He has bigger plans. God's agenda is to set us free from the bonds of self and the attitudes and mindsets poured in by family and experiences. His plans are greater, bigger, and higher than any strategy or scheme we've mapped out. He isn't interested in what we think we can be. He is interested in transforming every part of us, because God intends to make us like Christ. The question is, will I cling to little modifications, or will I allow total change? Will I embrace what He has arranged?

If you are like me when you read the paragraph above, you become a cheerleader for God. *Yes, God do something great in and with me. I want to be free and transformed. Yay, God!*

But we shrink back and sulk away when we discover that the transformation is accompanied by discouragement, which will always cause me to bargain for less—a lesser version of God's promises and a lesser solution to our difficulties.

When the Apostle Paul was held prisoner, the guards transported him by ship to Rome where he would face trial. Paul was accompanied by his friend and physician, Luke, as well as other political prisoners. The weather changed drastically when a nor'easter blew in. The crew tried every sailor's solution—sails lowered, life boats secured, sea anchor set, and ropes passed around the hull—to keep the boat from tearing apart. But the storm became more violent. The crew jettisoned the cargo and threw gear overboard. This catastrophic storm was a desperate moment in Paul's life. Paul had been through many difficult situations. He listed these troubles in a letter to the Corinthians.

"I have worked harder, been put in prison more often, been whipped times without number, and faced death again and again. Five different times the Jewish leaders gave me thirty-nine lashes. Three times I was beaten with rods. Once I was stoned. Three times I was shipwrecked. Once I spent a whole night and a day adrift at sea. I have traveled on many long journeys. I have faced danger from rivers and from robbers. I have faced danger from my own people, the Jews, as well as from the Gentiles. I have faced danger in the cities, in the deserts, and on the seas. And I have faced danger from men who claim to be believers but are not. I have worked hard and long, enduring many sleepless nights. I have been hungry and thirsty

and have often gone without food. I have shivered
in the cold, without enough clothing to keep me
warm" (2 Corinthians 11:23-27 TLB).

It doesn't seem that Paul listed these troubles to brag. Instead, he taught that it isn't the magnitude or the volume of our difficulty that matters. It is the faithfulness of God. Read what Paul said about his troubles,

"I think you ought to know, dear brothers, about
the hard time we went through in Asia. We were
really crushed and overwhelmed, and feared
we would never live through it. We felt we
were doomed to die and saw how powerless we
were to help ourselves; but that was good..." (2
Corinthians 1:8-9a TLB).

Wait! Stop right there. Did Paul say, "we felt we were doomed to die...but that was good?" Good? How could all that danger and turmoil be good?
Paul explained,

"For then we put everything into the hands of
God, who alone could save us, for he can even
raise the dead. And he did help us and saved us
from a terrible death; yes, and we expect him to
do it again and again"
(2 Corinthians 1:9b-10 TLB).

Imagine, facing doom and saying (believing) it was good. Paul could believe and say that word "good" because he knew when we have no hope, God is limitlessly powerful and radically faithful; He turns ends into beginnings and bad into good.

Once while traveling in Europe for business, I stayed at a hotel in Germany for several days. After returning home, I received a message from the hotel stating that I owed an amount on my bill. I found my credit card receipts showing I had already paid and responded.

Later that week I got a message from the hotel management written in broken English, "We sorry for bother about invoice and feel happy for your quick answer with the receipts. We apologize. We have moved our accountings to a different city and since then have had many trubbles."

The strange spelling and my southern pronunciation of "trubbles" (trroooobles) has become a mantra for my soul. When life is tough and I don't want to go on, I say to myself, *you have some trubbles!* And somehow saying the funny word makes my load lighter and my burden simpler.

The reason we can take trouble in stride, and even with humor, is because His faithfulness is great and never failing. Through His unfailing character, we are able to wrestle free from our failures.

Has discouragement caused you to settle for less?

Understanding God's faithfulness changes everything.

Remember that to God my troubles are only *trubbles.*

****

Oh, and that navy-blue quilt? My mom became my Abishai when she rescued the fabric and kit from the trash can, turning the discarded quilt into a family heirloom.

****

When you embrace God's faithfulness, you
become a giant killer.

When discouragement
overwhelms...

...our God
is faithful

Chapter 3
Fight for Your Life

God's plan for you is not to live in discouragement. Knowing that He is faithful and relying on that faithfulness will change your life forever and give you a new direction as you slay the giant of discouragement. God is not the God of the tweak; He is the God of transformation.[6] A tweak is getting along *somehow*. Transformation is slaying the giant of discouragement.

God's plans for you are to make you like Christ. Peter said,

> "The more you grow like this, the more productive and useful you will be in your knowledge of our Lord Jesus Christ"
> (2 Peter 1:8).

Paul said,

> "For God knew his people in advance, and he chose them to become like his Son"
> (Romans 8:29).

It's clear that these Apostles knew that God's plans are good.

Will you allow God to transform you, or will you settle for a tweak?

Jacob traveled with the family to see his twin brother Esau (Read the story in Genesis 32-33). The history of Esau and Jacob wasn't pretty. When Jacob and Esau were young boys living at home, their father favored Esau, and their mother preferred Jacob. (Maybe that's how Jacob learned to favor Joseph and Benjamin.) One day, Jacob cheated Esau out of his inheritance, and the brothers parted as bitter enemies. Now years later, they would meet again. Jacob, feeling guilty, brought gifts to appease Esau. These human efforts might tweak their relationship but wouldn't bring total peace.

Jacob received the report that Esau was on his way with 400 men. It didn't sound like a dinner-on-the-grounds family reunion. Jacob was afraid and couldn't sleep. In the night, a man came to Jacob. The two wrestled all night. Jacob would not let the man go until he gave Jacob a blessing (Genesis 32:24-26). Jacob fought back, defending himself, stubbornly refusing to give control until he realized the man was God.

Jacob seemed ready to settle for a tweak. *Save me from Esau!* But God fought for total transformation. All night they wrestled. Finally, God dislocated Jacob's hip. Imagine the pain. Then Jacob stopped relying on himself and trusted faithful God. God is faithful to rescue us—even from ourselves.

Some of us have allowed our health to deteriorate and now, we are out of breath, out of energy, and we feel weak and ill. We take a handful of pills each morning—some that treat the symptoms but don't cure the problem. We could exercise and build muscle and strength, but we swallow the tweak and don't try for the transformation.

Many of us are overweight. In fact, 40% of adults and 20% of children are obese in America. (Some reports indicate that the percentages may be even higher.) So, we try the next diet fad or drink diet shakes. We lose a little weight only to gain it back as soon as we go off the extreme diet. Dieting is a tweak. Lifestyle change—eating from all food groups in moderate amounts—transforms us into healthy, fit individuals.

Some of us have stubbornly refused to reconcile with another person because of a perceived injustice or how the person acted or what the person said. Saying you forgive them is a step forward, but it may only be a tweak. Transformation through forgiveness is more than words. Transformation means we get over our pride and instead reconcile with the person if we can. But to be truly transformed, pray for that person to be abundantly blessed by God. Pray that person will be successful in life and in ministry. When you pray like that, *you* will be freed.

Transformation also means walking in wisdom because we must withdraw from people who cannot be trusted—such as repeat abusers.

Too many of us are not following closely enough with God for transformation to happen. We go to church and we are involved in activities sponsored by the church, but we are like spectators. We haven't developed a personal intimacy with God. We think a seminar or conference will fix our spiritual deficiencies, but we discover the fix is simply a tweak. Spending time reading and meditating on God's Word and praying bring transformation.

Will you trust and obey our faithful God?

Like Jacob, I have wrestled God until I was exhausted. His love and determination for my transformation has staggered and constrained me until I decided to trust Him. Knowing

Him intimately is terrifying and thrilling, breathtaking and astonishing. He's never dull or boring. And He is always faithful.

After my job loss, we sold our dream home at a loss creating a debt that would take years to overcome. Silence from people I had considered friends overwhelmed me some days. My feelings of rejection were intense. I played the blame game and the pity-me game. I considered pursuing a lawsuit—as if I was throwing rocks at the people who hurt me. But I soon discovered two options: 1) I could live as some do, wallowing in the brokenness as if it is normal or 2) I could find a way to start over.

Day by day, God showed me He would be my provision and transformation.

Identity Loss

The problem for me, at first, was not about the loss of the job. I knew many who had survived downsizing and corporate turf wars. For me, the job loss was identity theft. If I'm not the successful vice president of a multi-national corporation, then who am I? If I'm not one of the first women in a tough male-dominated industry, then who am I? As I sat in my favorite chair, I didn't know who I was or what I would do. There was no place to go. The question wasn't, "Could I thrive?" It was, "Could Karen survive?"

When we built our dream home on the acreage in the woods, we used most of our savings and reserves to finish the house. We believed we could replenish the accounts quickly. The weekend before losing my job, we had purchased a new car. The monthly costs to pay the mortgage, replenish reserves, and maintain a household were huge—especially if I had no job. Facing these facts left me gasping for air. If we couldn't pay the bills, then what?

I'd never been that discouraged before, and it didn't feel right or good. I was young, healthy, and full of ideas and ability. But the loss of the job that identified me as a successful, powerful, corporate sensation sucked creativity and optimism right out of me. What if the job, the position, and the star power defined me as a person, too? Was there anything left after removing the trappings of Corporate Karen?

As I sat in the parched, hopeless desert of my life, the words of Psalm 118:17 stirred tiny embers buried beneath the pain.

Perhaps.

Somehow.

Could *I*...survive?

The verse not only said, *you will not die;* it also contained a hopeful promise.

"I will not die, but live" (Psalm 118:17).

David, the Psalmist, faced horrific circumstances—hostile nations surrounded; attacks that seemed like swarms of bees; enemies all around—yet he saw a bright beginning. Not death—life. In Psalm 118, David summed up the essence of hope. The words not only fanned the flame in me to fight back; the words also gave me the encouragement to live not die, stirring in me the idea of a fresh start.

I took the first baby steps from despair to hope—sometimes walking, sometimes wandering, and sometimes slogging. I rambled through the worry thickets, "How would we pay the bills?" I hid in the panic bushes mumbling, "No hope. No hope." I wondered about the power of God.

Do you worry about the future? Have you been slammed to the bottom? It's still and lonely there.

David Turned to God

I'm sure David had many counselors and friends he could have consulted, but David turned to God. David needed relief and discovered deliverance only comes from God.

When I call, give me answers. God, take my side! (Psalm 4:1 The Message).

Like David, I needed God to take my side. If I would survive or if I would ever get up from the bottom, I needed Him. I needed transformation.

In his Psalms, David seemed quick to go to God. Me? Not so much.

I talked to lawyers, clients, leaders in my industry, family members, friends, but I couldn't find relief. Many of them, especially my children, were as angry and hurt as I was.

David seemed to understand that with God, we will gain victory. Perhaps because of his failures and times of rebellion. As I read David's words, I wondered if I could get to the point of trusting God like he did. Could I stop blaming the foreigners who bought the company, the president who didn't protect me, the current state of affairs in corporate America, and the laws that failed to rescue me from ruthless managers, or even my bad luck? If I could only stop the blame game and start the claim game; if I could get away from the stigma and concerns of my bad luck and claim God as my victor. Then I would live!

My steps took me to the brink with this question, "Is the loss of my job, position, power, and prestige the end?"

What is your question?

Is losing my loved one the end of me?

Can I pick up the pieces after divorce?

Will I recover from the huge mistake I made?

Can I leave my addiction behind?

For me, the answer appeared bit by bit. As light exchanges shadow with the early morning sunrise, anticipation replaced despair. Optimism superseded pessimism. Faith traded places with loss. Desire dissolved apathy. Hope birthed in me. Transformation began because God is faithful.

The journey from tweak to transformation required a slow process of putting one foot in front of the other.

Chapter 4
What's a Girl to Do...

Following in the steps of God requires courage. God will provide the courage.

You have to take one step. And then another.

Walk away from what causes anguish.

Walk toward what creates and gives life.

Your pursuit of obeying God is the beginning of a miracle. The miracle of the steps.

But it's scary. The path before us looks like a thick forest filled with bushes, trees, limbs, and twisted vines. There is no obvious trail, or at least we can't see it. We can't see the good or the bad waiting ahead. The view may be great beyond the tangled undergrowth or danger could lurk in the darkness of the next bend. We don't know. We can't see.

But as we follow God, we lift our foot, gather our courage, and take the next step—somehow. He opens the way enough for one step. Then we take the next step, and it becomes clear too—but only when we actually take the step. So, the journey can feel slow and scary and requires us to keep taking steps. With God's help, and because we trust His faithfulness, we keep moving.

Sometimes we step into the familiar. Sometimes we step into the unfamiliar.

What circumstances have led you to face the giant of discouragement?

The *miracle* of the steps only becomes most clearly seen when we turn around and look where we've been. We discover the path behind us is not a tangled web of obstacles. Instead it is a lighted highway—smooth and wide with signposts along the way. Even if we missed some of the signs, He makes a path when there seems to be no trail. David understood the concept when he praised God for ordering his steps.

"You gave a wide place for my steps under me,
and my feet did not slip" (Psalm 18:36).

Maybe the discouraged situation you are in today—that terrible problem that has you looking up from the bottom—is nothing more than a stepping stone to the transformation God is dreaming for you. God knows the past, present, and future, and His faithfulness will show you what to do next.

David also proclaimed how God had made his feet "as surefooted as a deer" (Psalm 18:33). A deer doesn't stumble on rocks or get tangled in vines. A deer's feet glide over the stumbling places. When God orders our steps, we can navigate the rough patches.

Nothing in my life has ever been about vulnerability and candor. Not as a teen when my goal was to break free from the rules. Or as an adult—keeping up appearances with the neighbors, with the church folk, with building a persona at the office—all the while building my reputation as the perfect mother, the perfect wife, the great executive, the best hostess, the neatest housekeeper, the uniquely clever decorator, and the impressive gourmet cook. As the '80's commercial promised, "I could bring home the bacon and fry it up in a pan."

I even made lists of all the jobs I performed: housekeeper, cook, chauffeur, nurse, teacher, counselor, friend, Bible teacher, executive, writing coach, speaker, mentor, mother, wife, lover… the list was endless. When people commented on all I could do, I'd smile demurely, but underneath I cheered, "Yes I can do it all!"

Have you ever felt secure in yourself like I did? If so, what discouragements did you face? If not, describe your feelings.

The Raw Truth

As I think about those lists and the moments of self-importance, I'm shocked at my pride and false bravado. I never set out to be a prideful person. Some of what I felt was true. I love my family above all other things. My daughter and son and their families are the heartbeat of my life. I adore them. I love my husband to a fault. I love the Lord, and I love the Bible. These facts are true and totally without question.

But my emphasis was on being perfect.

The kids needed to look great, act great, have lofty dreams, be successful, and keep their rooms neat. The husband needed to go along with all my plans and watch me adoringly as I bulldozed my way through the world. And while the Bible never failed to give me comfort and encouragement, it was often useful to show off my skills in teaching and organizing at church—especially if someone near me in church could see how much marking I'd done in the margins of my well-worn Bible. *Surely, they would know how deeply spiritual I am.* My love for family and God was real, but my manipulation of each one contributed to my need to look good. The rest—the job, and eventually the writing and speaking—piled on like some fifty-car-freeway pile-up on a foggy morning. And what a wreck it was!

Consider what might be your first steps toward transformation. Write these goals here. How will each one help you slay the giant of discouragement?

Get a Job

Let's go back to the beginning. How did I get to that big executive desk? It started in early marriage when our children were under seven years old.

My husband and I had the conversation one Sunday afternoon while the kids napped, and we struggled with the household finances. We'd recently bought our first home. How we got the loan in the first place was incredulous, and the idea that we could make a house payment was ludicrous to us. So, we talked.

"The cost of closing and moving was much more than I thought it would be," he said.

"And there is so much I need to do to the house to decorate and make it beautiful," I said.

"But there's no extra money for that now."

"But your new job is great, and you'll get bonuses. Besides we have the company car now."

"Yeah, but can we make it to the first bonus?"

"Maybe I should get a job."

"What if you worked for a few months to get us over the struggles of the move?"

"I can do that! I'll start looking for a job tomorrow."

I'm sure many young couples have had the same kind of conversation. Money is tight. The cars need repair. The kids need clothes. Items for the house would be nice. Then there's always travel and food on the table.

So, we made the big decision. I had wanted to stay home and be with the kids when they were small, but I would go to work for a little while. I knew I could get a job quickly, and I could make enough to help us get over the financial challenges.

When you look back, what mindsets and attitudes set you up for discouragement?

The job offer came quickly. A gregarious guy hired me as his assistant in a food company. I moved into my small office adjacent to his and began to learn. The business was grain; the company was an interesting combination of a modified farmers co-op, a huge mill located near downtown, and a consumer sales group both domestic and international. I worked hard and learned fast. My boss had been a buyer of the raw product (truckloads of harvested grain the farmers sent to the mill). He had little interest in being VP of International Sales but somehow had been pushed into the position because the previous VP of sales had left the company. One of the company's biggest markets was the Middle East, and he was slated to take a market survey trip there. He didn't relish the thought.

His dislike of travel and for the management position won the battle one morning. He resigned. That same day the executive assistant to the president of the company walked out. I guess I should have known that something wasn't good about the situation in the office, but I ignored the warning sign of three key people resigning within such a short time.

I kept coming to work.

One morning my phone rang. It was the general manager of the company who told me to move into the office adjacent to his because I would now be his executive assistant. He was in his car. Calling from the car seems commonplace now but then, no one owned personal cell phones. He had one of the early mobile devices. Huge. Clunky. And we used the words *over* and *out* at the end of the call.

I moved to his assistant's office and settled in.

When he arrived, I got a taste of this powerful and remarkable man's management style. As he walked past my door, he said, "Come into my office." I had only met him once before this so I felt a little intimidated.

He reached into his briefcase and pulled out a stack of yellow pages. The stack was a long list of jobs to get done—his idea of managing the company in his unusual administrative style. His organizational chart was simple. He was at the top, and there was one line beneath his name with everyone else's name on that line. He micro-managed every person from the highest-level executive to the paid-by-the-hour employee in the warehouse. Everyone answered to him.

He was good at leading and keeping up with people and projects, and when I became his executive assistant, I got to know everyone and everything. I worked hard. He began to trust me. Soon I was helping manage some of the areas of the company— at least I knew where all the keys were.

Within a couple of years, a new corporation bought the company, ousted the general manager, and a new group of executives piled into the offices. Since I knew where everything was, they kept me. I cooperated and worked hard. Within a few months, the president of the new corporation gave me a big raise and a promotion into the international marketing department. From that moment, I was hooked on the business, on the position, on the excitement, on the money, on the power that came with a corporate position. I went from getting a temporary job to a new idea for my future.

What is your story and where is the turning point? Can you see how you pursued the future without God?

My Journey

I was born into a middle-class family; maybe lower-middle class is a better description. Money was neither abundant nor terribly scarce. At least I was never aware of it. I knew we weren't rich but it didn't seem to matter much. No one we knew was rich either except maybe the parents of my high school friend, who had built the biggest swimming pool I'd ever seen.

My parents loved God and loved the church with a great passion. Mother and Daddy had lived through the brown, dry days of the Great Depression. Daddy worked in the oil fields and any other job where hard work was required. Outgoing, extroverted, expressive, and highly-opinionated, he lived a rowdy life until he met Jesus in the 1940s.

My parent's journey to Christ began a few years after my brother was born. Mom became pregnant again. They were delighted when their little girl, Kathryn Adaline, was born. Within minutes of the birth, the doctors delivered a stillborn twin. Without the benefit of ultra sound and other tests, the doctors had no way of knowing Mother had conceived twins or that one of the babies had only survived a few months of the pregnancy. In a few days, complications from the trauma also took Kathryn's life.

Heartbroken, their previous lifestyle no longer interested my parents. Daddy's father, my grandfather, suggested they go to a revival meeting. There, my parents learned that Jesus offered healing for their pain. From then on, Daddy and Mother lived their new-found Christianity with abandon. Church was everything; Bible study was paramount. Church people were friends now. We went to church twice on Sunday and on Wednesday evening and any other time the doors were open. Week nights, they studied the Bible; Sunday, they taught classes. There were rules and more rules—mostly what we weren't allowed to do.

Our church belonged to one of the more than 250 different kinds of Baptists and was so conservative that we were taught that other denominations, even other Baptists, were too liberal and should be avoided at all costs. And these teachings were adamant and strong and you didn't dare cross them and you certainly didn't ask questions.

Did experiences in your early life affect your personality and feelings or your view of God?

Work Hard

Daddy believed in hard work. He worked so hard that sweat would drip from his face following a line down his large nose to the tip where the drop would hang for what seemed like hours before it would fall. That drop captivated me as I waited for it to let loose. Daddy worked intently, and he taught us to always work hard. I believed in his work ethic, and whether I inherited it from him as what we call the "family gene" or whether it was a product of being around him, I am a worker, too. I translated his work-hard code to my personal, yet flawed, set of beliefs. *If I work hard enough, good things will happen to me. If I work hard, everyone will be pleased with me. Daddy. Mom. God.*

Look Good

Mother was a gentle and loving person with great talents and a heart for all things decent and in order. Her life was centered on making our lives better. She beautifully decorated our home on a tiny budget. She made my clothes with such creativity and pizzazz that I was always stylishly dressed. She wanted us to look good to the world around us and to the church that we associated with. So, we did. And while she didn't actually teach me to play a fake role in life, I translated and twisted her authentically good traits into my own version of look-good-no-matter-what life philosophy; look good even if things are rotten inside.

Mother was genuinely good, but I got the wrong message. I thought the most important value was the outward show. Be perfect, beautiful, and all together.

I Created a Fiction

As a corporate skyrocket and one of the first women in my particular industry, I thrived. I carried the energy and success into my church life as the I-Can-Do-It Church Lady—not to mention the continued quest to be the perfect wife and mother and hostess. I accomplished it all by developing a stack-and-pile method of dealing with problems and a rake-and-conquer method of house cleaning. It became a fantasy of perfection I created.

What fiction have you created?

God wants a relationship not busyness. He doesn't care how much you do *for* Him if you have no intimate connection *with* Him. You can build your intimacy with Him one step at a time. Begin with a verse or two each day. Start with a prayer you read from a book. Write one sentence in a journal expressing your love and gratitude. As you take steps, He walks with you and soon your heart and His will be bonded together.

It is the miracle of the steps.

Giant 2

Defeat

Chapter 5
The Giant

I s it possible to face a giant more cruel than discouragement? I know it's hard to believe because discouragement takes us lower than low.

Let's go back to David's camp to find out what happened next. After Abishai, who represents the faithfulness of God, killed the giant of discouragement, Saph, another of Goliath's brothers, came looking for a fight.

> "After this, there was another battle against the
> Philistines at Gob. As they fought, Sibbecai
> from Hushah killed Saph, another descendant
> of the giants" (2 Samuel 21:18).

His name is Saph. His name means destroyer.

He is the terminator.

He shouts words like, "You will never win."

And "You will never be victorious."

Saph is the giant of defeat.

What's the difference between discouragement and defeat? One knocks you down; the other knocks you out.

Defeat is the knock-out punch.

It feels as if I face Saph, the giant of defeat, every week when I can't finish all I began, and it seems I'm farther behind than ever. My to-do list grows, my bank account shrinks, and the bills multiply. *When will it all collapse?*

I face the giant of defeat when I make progress getting along with that self-focused person only to experience a gut-punch because of the latest insult she slipped in sideways.

The giant of defeat jabs at me when I haven't made those phone calls or sent those cards. That hulking giant looms over my desk. *You are a failure.*

Defeat convinces me that I can't ever come out of this mess I've made.

Defeat happens on so many levels. Perhaps you have been trying to reach someone, a family member for example, who needs Christ. You've tried every conversation and lifestyle idea but the person has not responded. And it seems they never will.

Perhaps your feelings were hurt in some way, and you cannot let it go. You want to forgive and move on, but the pain rises up in your mind, defeating you when you lay your head on the pillow at night.

Maybe the doctor has given you a diagnosis like cancer or some other scary illness. You'll have to endure treatments that make you sick, and the giant reminds you that your days on earth are limited. He whispers, *you lose, I win.*

We can't seem to keep defeat from settling into our hearts and minds.

After that job-loss day in the office of my beautiful home and reading Psalm 118:17, I stepped triumphantly on the chest of the first slain giant, the giant of discouragement. I thought, *I can trust God's faithfulness, and we'll make it through.* I believed, and I took action to move forward because of God's faithfulness.

But the enemy wouldn't leave me alone. He sent the giant of defeat.

In the weeks following my job loss, we decided we would have to sell the house. We put it on the market as the real estate prices in our area took a downturn. We finally sold the house—at a loss. In fact, we took out a loan so we could make the sale.

We determined that we would move to the south side of town, some 75 miles away. Our daughter and her husband and three of our grandbabies were in that area. So, it made sense to us to move there. We searched for a house to rent. The rental market boomeranged from out-of-repair houses to out-of-our-price-range houses, with little in between. We were in no condition emotionally or mentally or financially to find something permanent. In my crushed condition, rental houses were the wisest option.

Relief washed over me when we finally found a reasonably priced house in a nice neighborhood. It was small but we took all our stuff. Imagine, we moved *all* the furniture and goods from that big house in the woods to the little rent house. The movers must have laughed, but they made a maze, a trail through the boxes so we could move from one room to the other. Some bedrooms had furniture and boxes stacked to the ceiling.

We continued to live in one room of our dream home for several more weeks while we wrapped up the loose ends and allowed my husband, who was a teacher, to finish the semester. On the Friday before a holiday weekend, I traveled to the rent house to begin sorting through boxes.

I wandered through the box-maze into the laundry-utility room. In there, we had a large upright freezer that was full of food. I opened the door to discover that the freezer was warm, and the food inside was ruined. We learned later that the plug the movers had plugged the freezer into was defective.

I was alone in a part of town I didn't know with our large freezer full of ruined meat and other foods—on a holiday weekend. I called the city office only to learn that the trash service wouldn't be there until after the holidays. The man gave me the phone number of 5 landfills in the near vicinity. I called the first, which didn't take food items. I called 3 others to learn they were closed because of the holiday. I called the last one, which was located in a small town a few miles away. Yes, they would take it, but I needed to hurry to get there before closing time.

I found a box of big black garbage bags to fill with warm packages of squishy meat. I loaded multiple heavy bags into my car and drove to the landfill facility.

When I arrived, I saw a long straight road leading to the tall land-fill mound. I envisioned some nice young man unloading my bags, and I could be on my way. Instead, at the end of the road was a small security shack with serious gatekeepers. First, they charged me $45 to leave my trash bags, and then they said I could drive down to the far end of the road (down where the big black birds were circling) and toss my bags over the wall.

I live in south Texas and the temperature that day was somewhere around 175 degrees—at least it felt that way. I opened the back of my car and dragged the heavy bags over to the wall and lifted them up and over. "Splat."

When I finally dumped the last bag over the wall, I got back into my car and laid my sweaty face on the steering wheel. And then I cried. I screamed. I complained. The giant of defeat moved closer to hiss wicked words in my ear, "Why didn't you check the plug? How could you waste so much food? They fired you. You won't make it. Don't you see that there's no hope for you?"

I—who had been on a first-name basis with heads of state, broken the glass ceiling in my industry, worked in a wonderful private office in a high-rise office building, and supervised a staff working for me—was at the dump, covered in simmering meat juices on the hottest day of the year.

I had no prospects for the future. No dreams of what I might be able to do with my life next.

Beaten.

Crushed.

Utterly Defeated.

Defeat is more than being blocked or slowed down. It is more than dragging an anchor. Defeat is collapse—demoralized beyond the point of redemption. More than obstructed. More than crushed or overwhelmed. Defeated.

Defeat feels as if you don't deserve a chance because you aren't good enough. You feel you probably couldn't make it—even if you were given a chance.

The danger of defeat is no hope.

No will to go on.

The books say to get exercise, pull yourself out, save yourself, know your identity, change your attitude. Advisors say, *take charge of your life and stop feeling bad. Look on the bright side and always wear a smile.* But when the giant of defeat shows up, you become exhausted from trying so hard to be stronger than you feel. You'd like to curl up in a ball in the corner and suck your thumb.

Defeat Attacks the Best Among Us

As a young man, Abraham Lincoln went to war a captain and returned a private. He failed as a businessman and lawyer. He was defeated in his first try at politics and his second and his third and his fourth, including legislature, commissioner, senate, and vice president. He wrote, "I am now the most miserable man living. If what I feel were equally distributed to the whole human family, there would not be one cheerful face on the earth." Piled onto Lincoln's feelings of defeat, the media were relentless in mocking his early days as President. A tour of his Presidential library begins with thousands of critical cartoons about him— depicting him as a buffoon and worse.

Winston Churchill excelled at certain subjects while doing dismally in others. He repeated a grade during elementary school. When he took exams to enter Harrow School at about age 12, he was placed in the lowest division of the lowest class. Later, he twice failed the entrance exam to the Royal Military Academy at Sandhurst. Churchill was defeated in his first effort to serve in Parliament.

Sigmund Freud was booed from the podium when he first presented his ideas to the scientific community of Europe.

Thomas Edison's teachers said he was "too stupid to learn anything." He was fired from his first two jobs for being "non-productive." As an inventor, Edison made 1,000 unsuccessful attempts to invent the light bulb.

Albert Einstein reportedly did not speak until he was 4-years-old and did not read until he was 7. His parents thought he was "sub-normal," and one of his teachers described him as "mentally slow, unsociable, and adrift forever in foolish dreams." He was expelled from school and was refused admittance to the Zurich Polytechnic School.

Louis Pasteur was only a mediocre pupil in undergraduate studies and ranked 15th out of 22 students in chemistry. In 1872, Pierre Pachet, Professor of Physiology at Toulouse, wrote that "Louis Pasteur's theory of germs is ridiculous fiction."

Henry Ford, creator of the assembly line technique of mass production, went broke five times.

Fred Smith, the founder of Federal Express, received a C on his college paper detailing his idea for a reliable overnight delivery service. His professor at Yale told him, "Well, Fred, the concept is interesting and well formed, but in order to earn better than a C grade, your ideas also have to be feasible."

Walt Disney was fired by a newspaper editor because, "He lacked imagination and had no good ideas."

Enrico Caruso's music teacher said he had no voice at all and could not sing. His parents wanted him to become an engineer.

Decca Records turned down a recording contract with the Beatles saying, "We don't like their sound. Groups with guitars are on their way out."

In 1954, Jimmy Denny, manager of the Grand Ole Opry, fired Elvis Presley after one performance. He told Presley, "You ain't goin' nowhere, son. You ought to go back to drivin' a truck."

Each of these men heard the giant of defeat, the one who says we'll never amount to anything no matter how hard we try.

Sharon's Story

Sharon knew she would never be able to tell her family and friends the secret she kept locked away. Especially not the family she now claimed as hers. They were religious. She wasn't complaining because she loved every straight-laced minute she'd experienced as part of Jim's family since her marriage. She loved the food and the meals around the big table. She loved the laughter and the teasing. She had come to love the small church with its beautiful songs and sermons—especially since she had made the decision to follow Jesus Christ. Sharon's childhood had been nothing like this. The stability in her childhood was her tiny great grandmother who spoke sweet words of comfort even though she had little money or other resources. As a teen, Sharon loved this precious woman but found the little house to be boring. Sharon ran with a daring crowd and dropped out of school. She gave birth to her son and then to her daughter. Her life consisted of parties, while her babies stayed with their great grandmother.

Around her now-family, Sharon was drug and alcohol free and happily raising her first two children along with her new husband's kids. Sharon felt safe with these people who loved her. No one knew her secret that she had never finished high school. No one knew the regret she carried under the façade of her smile. No one knew that she wanted to get a job but without a high school diploma, she couldn't. No one knew that in her heart, she carried a hidden dream. She wanted to be a nurse. Not much chance of that since she had no credentials and no hope of getting any. She dove deeper into defeat.

We live in defeat because we don't believe God will help us.
What is your defeat?
Is it physical—weight or health?
Is it relational—marriage, children?
Is it vocational—job and dreams?
Is it emotional—memories and pain?
Is it spiritual—ministry or relationship with God?

Chapter 6
The Weapon

What have your discarded as an impossible dream? Do you feel as if you can't get up? Not one more time. Not ever. That's how I felt. Defeated.

I couldn't cling to my faith because it felt as if God had abandoned me. I didn't have the strength. I couldn't rely on my achievements because my identity as Corporate Karen was gone. Not one solution that would make life okay. No job or prospects. Honestly no desire to find a job. Not a friend to call. My family fumed at the injustice done to me.

Though he tried not to show it, my husband's shock was equal to mine. The intimacy of him sharing this journey was a gift I didn't know how to appreciate. I simply sat in the hot Texas sun with my head on the steering wheel of my SUV. It felt like defeat. I felt like dying.

And I likely could have died in that heat, if I'd stayed there much longer with the windows up. Thankfully the dump was about to close so I had to turn on my AC and drive out of there.

When Saph, the giant of defeat, entered David's camp, one of David's mighty men rose up sword in hand.

This mighty man's name was Sibbecai, which means to entwine or fold together. His name represents how God entwines himself with us. Even in our most defeated moments, God supernaturally intervenes.

The supernatural entwining or intervention of God is the only way to face the giant of defeat. Only God offers control when we are out of control. His Spirit changes our hearts. He changes hate and hopelessness, to love and forgiveness.

When the children of Israel faced enemies that seemed impossible to beat, Moses said,

> "For the Lord your God is going with you! He will fight for you against your enemies, and he will give you victory" (Deuteronomy 20:4).

The people had assumed defeat before the battle began and they would have been severely beaten except that God intervened in the battle and won the victory.

When you are in the throes of defeat as I was that day in the car at the town dump, you can't think of any answers. The future looked impossible. The Israelites felt that way. Sometimes, the disciples felt that way, too.

Jesus assured them,

> "Humanly speaking, it is impossible, but with God everything is possible" (Matthew 19:26).

God is able to rescue us from defeat. He loves to give us triumph. When we are in the trap of defeat, he reaches down and entwines Himself with us. Sometimes He changes situations, lives, hearts, minds, and actions. He supernaturally intervenes. Rescue is not automatic of course—I can hear you countering with examples when the situation did not change. The illness persisted. The cruel one triumphed. The disability remained. And you are right. If God doesn't change your situation immediately, don't think that God loves you any less or is ignoring you. This world delivers many injustices, largely because of the presence of free will. But no matter what, God will show you what to do as you walk through it. God will cry with you. You will never, ever be alone. He will renew your heart and mind (Philippians 4:7; Hebrews 8:10). He will move you from heartache into joy. He will send light into your darkness.

God did not swoop down to give me my job or my home back. Instead, He went with me as I drove to the rental house and tried to set order to the boxes. I became more and more despondent because there was not enough room for all the stuff. Then I noticed that the rent house was beige. You may not find beige unusual, but the colorlessness rose up like a bully. The walls and ceiling were beige. The cabinets were beige. The windows were beige. The counter tops were beige. The carpet and tile were beige. Beige everywhere.

My dream home had been a display of color. The walls were sunshine yellow! Each room had a color theme...red, blue, purple, or coral...and it worked because every color goes with "sunshine." I thrive on color and patterns and textures in my home.

But this house was beige. I wish you could hear me say it, "Beiiiiiigggggg."

I asked George if we could get some flowers to put in the front flower beds so that as I entered the house, there would be a color splash. We bought some containers of colorful annuals to fill the flower bed. Late that afternoon, we got on our hands and knees to plant the flowers.

I need to stop here and tell you how we looked. Imagine how grubby we were from working inside the house all day cleaning and moving boxes. I was a special mess because I had put on a hair band early that morning and let my hair fly free pushed back from my face. I have extremely curly—read frizzy—hair so by that afternoon, the frizz was sticking up out of that hair band like some tangled mop. But I was planting colorful flowers, so I was happy.

As we dug in the dirt, we heard the door open next door. Out came our new neighbor. He skipped up our sidewalk and introduced himself. We later dubbed him "Happy Larry" because he was so gregarious and buoyant.

Because I was covered in grime, I was embarrassed, but even worse was when he asked, "What do you do?" I had no answer. I had lost my identity with the loss of my job. I couldn't think of how to answer. I believed I didn't *do* anything.

Defeat.

I blurted out the words, "I'm a writer." Now, I think that answer is funny and a little bit prophetic, but then I thought, *you are so stupid.*

Then Happy Larry asked George, "What do you do?"

"I'm a teacher." George answered.

"Where do you teach?"

"Right now, I'm teaching at a school up north about 75 miles from here, but I'm hoping to find a teaching job here."

"Really? What do you teach?"

"Seventh and eighth grade science."

Larry pulled his cell phone from his pocket and punched in a number. "Well that's amazing," he said, "My wife's best friend is principal of the junior high nearby, and she's looking for a science teacher."

And the next morning, George had a new teaching job.

A miracle? A divine intervention? I believe the answer is yes. That beige rent house that needed flowers. That curious neighbor.

In that moment, God whispered, "Karen, I always win over defeat."

Have you experienced the supernatural intervention of God? Has He shown up when you had no hope?

We are often defeated because we don't believe he will intervene. Yet, we are constantly surrounded by divine intervention.

We tend toward two extreme camps when it comes to divine intervention.

1). We deny. We take a scientific or human-only

logical reasoning and no matter what happens, we refuse to think that God is able to intervene or do miracles.

2). We see a miracle in everything. Nothing is too small for these miracle-everywhere people. A parking space opens up. A cloud looks like Jesus. The way the peanut butter sits on toast. All miracles.

Which is the truth? The first extreme is true: God definitely intervenes in our lives. He causes everything. He guides thinking and decisions. The second extreme is true as well: He suspends the rules of nature and steps outside the norm. There are miracles, healings, signs, and random interventions everywhere. However, we are not instructed to see signs in every detail of life nor are we to try to decode secret messages of clouds or peanut butter. The way out of defeat is to believe and know nothing stops God from His supernatural touch. That when we are at our worst place— utter defeat—He *will* interrupt our lives with His supernatural touch.

Here are a few examples of Divine intervention from the Bible.

Example 1

In 2 Chronicles 20, there is a remarkable story that illustrates how God intervenes. King Jehoshaphat was terrified by the news that a vast army from Edom was marching to fight the nation of Judah. The king prayed aloud before the entire community, calling on God to rescue. A prophet of God told the people,

> "March out and take your stand—You will not even need to fight" (20:17).

So, with faith in God and in the face of sure defeat, the people sang worship songs, giving praise and thanksgiving. At the moment the singing started, the armies who threatened them began fighting among themselves. They destroyed each other.

When the army of Judah arrived, there was not an enemy warrior to be seen. All they had to do was collect the plunder. They named the place the Valley of Blessing. Instead of defeat, God intervened, and they received blessing.

Example 2

Daniel and his friends Shadrach, Meshach, and Abednego were bright and capable young men who lived most of their lives in captivity but built trust and rose to leadership. Their integrity appeared to threaten other leaders. In one ploy to unseat them, these officials arranged for Daniel's three friends to be thrown into a fiery furnace. Later that day, King Nebuchadnezzar shouted,

> "I see four men, unbound, walking around in the fire unharmed! And the fourth looks like a god!" (Daniel 3:25).

God showed up and protected the boys from the fire. Intervention.

Example 3

Since God can see the end from the beginning, He saw through all history that humans would sin and create hopelessness. People would become lost and defeated and have no way out. God decided to physically intervene. He came to earth to show us how to live and what to do.

God sent an angel to Mary. The angel said, "[You] will bear a son and you shall call him Jesus" (Matthew 1:21). That son was Jesus the Christ, fully God and fully human, who lived a perfect 33-year-long life and then gave Himself to bear our sin on the cross. Intervening so that we would not have to pay the cost for our sins. He died so we wouldn't be required to die.

Paul said,

"But God showed His great love for us by
sending Christ to die for us while we were still
sinners" (Romans 5:8).

Thankfully, Jesus' death was not the end of God's amazing ultimate intervention. Though death appeared as defeat, His death led to victory. Jesus was raised from the tomb on the third day to live and never die again. Your death can also end in life. God intervenes with love, mercy, and grace so that anyone who believes will be saved.

"But thank God! He gives us victory over sin
and death through our Lord Jesus Christ"
(1 Corinthians 15:57).

Remember Sharon from last chapter? One day she told her friend about not graduating from high school and her dream of becoming a nurse. The friend encouraged Sharon to allow God to change her life. After that Sharon saw an ad for a course at a nearby school for those who wanted to pursue the GED diploma. Sharon wanted to attend but didn't want to tell her new family the truth.

One Sunday morning, the pastor spoke from Jeremiah.

"This is the word that came to Jeremiah from
the LORD: 'Go down to the potter's house,
and there I will give you my message.' So, I
went down to the potter's house, and I saw
him working at the wheel. But the pot he
was shaping from the clay was marred in his
hands; so, the potter formed it into another pot,
shaping it as seemed best to him"
(Jeremiah 18: 1-4 NIV).

Through the words of the verses and the pastor, Sharon saw God's role in her life in a new way. She understood that we never are so marred that God refuses to shape us some more. And everyone still needs shaping. Sharon was not alone in that. Sharon knew that with God's help, she could move forward to her dream. She found the courage to tell the truth and take action—she took the course and received her GED. Then she entered the local junior college to take the classes she needed to get into nursing school. Within a few years, she had received her LVN certification and a new job at the area's largest hospital. Sharon remembered the words from Jeremiah 18:4, "shaping it as it seemed best to him." She knew God would take care of her. Sharon enrolled again in nursing school and earned her RN degree.

Her progress became so dramatic that the nursing school offered her a teaching position. From eighth grade dropout to college professor. Impressive. She turned down the offer to teach so she could continue direct patient care. Sharon said, "God used me as a 9th grade dropout to touch other people. A kind word. A gentle touch. A Scripture."

God is never satisfied with a tweak or a bit of a change; He is planning our all-out, spectacular, transformation as he did for Sharon.

Ask for God's supernatural intervention. He never wants you to feel defeated, but the enemy does. God supernaturally intervenes with miracles and events to take us from defeat into victory.

Is there a place where you feel defeated?

> Finances
>
> Relationships
>
> Circumstances
>
> Weight
>
> Health
>
> Marriage
>
> Children
>
> Job
>
> Ministry

The key to receiving God's supernatural intervention is surrender. When we surrender to Him, we acknowledge that we need divine intervention. Will you now pray with me for God's supernatural intervention? If you do, keep your eyes open because He will entwine His power into your life and rock your world.

Impossible is not a word for God. He makes the impossible, possible.

When defeat crushes...

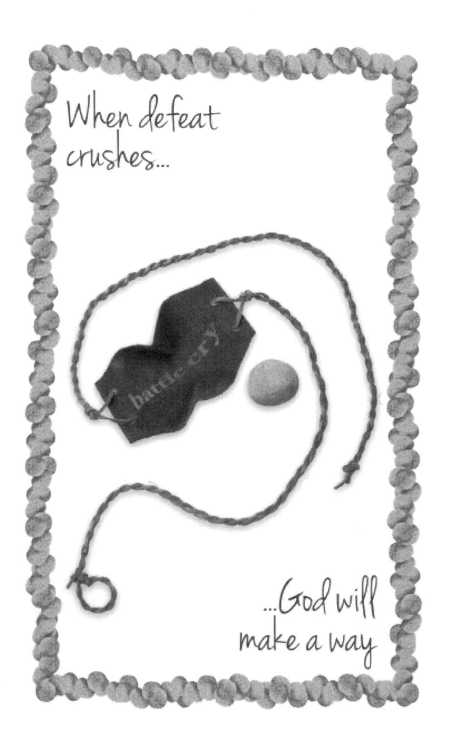

...God will make a way

Chapter 7
Fight for Your Life

My husband and I still faced difficulties and pain ahead. Selling the house for a huge loss and taking a loan to pay the difference. Moving to a rental house. Job search. Uncertainty. But hope now drove us. We would not die, but live! (Psalm 118:17).

Have you lost hope? Does it seem impossible for anything good to come out of your situation? Do you feel crushed and pinned down by your circumstances or your mistakes? Then I have good news for you. There is hope. There are wide-open spaces of possibility in your future. I know hope. Not because I found a verse that encouraged me. Not because I have an unrealistic view of life. Not because I'm hopelessly romantic. I know this hope because I know the One who is the giver of hope. He invented hope. He is the keeper and sustainer of hope. He is Jesus Christ. He is hope.

Without Jesus, hope is only wishful thinking and dreaming. Without Jesus, hope is only desire and yearning. Hope can be limited to goals and objectives—nothing more than hope-so.

With Jesus, hope is certain. Guaranteed. Hope is confidence not rooted in self-confidence but embedded in the undeniable, genuine God who cannot fail. God is all knowing, all perceptive, all understanding, all aware, and all sensitive. God never hesitates or staggers. He never gets tripped up. He never loses interest in us.

This God of hope is why David could write psalms about his enemies and their strength and about his own failures and faults and then say, "I will not die but live."

David could ask God,

> "Why have you forgotten me? Why must I go about mourning, oppressed by the enemy?" (Psalm 42:9).

He could talk about his suffering in terms of physical and emotional pain,

> "My bones suffer mortal agony as my foes taunt me, saying to me all day long, 'Where is your God? Why are you downcast, O my soul? Why so disturbed within me?'"

Then in the next breath, he could say with great assurance,

> "I will yet praise him..." (Psalm 42:9-11).

David lived the uneasy mix of pain coupled with faith. The two really can live together, because faith shows us confidence is a picture of hope. David knew that no matter how bad life gets, God is faithful.

You can have this confidence too—for with God, hope is not hope-so.

You may think you can't come out of your personal agony so easily. You may feel as if your pain is too hard. That God has let you down or forgotten you. Like David.

But I tell you without doubt and that no matter how you feel, God is faithful and He will intervene in your life.

Hope is More than Trying

We hope the stock market stays strong. We hope our team wins. We hope gas prices go down. We hope our children succeed in school and in life. We hope our spouse remains faithful. We hope for health. These are all *hope-so* hopes.

Our crippled culture needs wide-open hope not closed in hope-so. Authentic believers move in the power of hope. Our message to our neighbors and to our nation is that there is wide-open hope.

We all want to believe that if we have courage and if we work hard, we will receive a better life. And to some extent, we will. But living fully in spite of discouragement isn't by our courage or tenacity alone—that's only hope-so. Real hope happens when we partner with Jesus and break into the wide-open spaces he has made for us. The Bible says that God

> "...loved us and by his grace gave us eternal
> encouragement and good hope"
> (2 Thessalonians 2:16-17).

He sustains us even if we lose our job or the market takes a downturn. He cares about our lives no matter how much daily necessities cost. He watches over our children and promises that they will return to the truth even if they take a behavior detour. He's there even if it seems He is far. He is healer in sickness and cheerleader in health.

Hope-so—*invented hope*—is like a river rushing by. It may even be beautiful and powerful but it moves. I can't grasp flowing water. But wide-open hope is like a blue water lake with green mountains all around—serene, beautiful, rich, deep, and waiting for me to dive in.

For all those years in the corporate world, I hoped my abilities as an executive and my hard work would lead to company perks. I hoped in people—my boss, the owners, my clients, my co-workers. And they failed me. But when I placed my hope in Jesus, I found bona fide hope. It's not only true hope, it knows no boundaries. Wide open. Stretching farther than I can think or imagine.

In ancient Jerusalem, there was a crippled man. Kind souls carried him to the gate named Beautiful every day to beg for money. The man had no hope for a way to make a living. He had no hope for marriage or family. He was resigned to a life begging at the gate. Then one day Peter and John walked by. Though they had no money for his begging cup, they offered him the one thing he thought he could never have—the ability to walk. Hope! Peter reached out and lifted the man up. He walked for the first time in his life. From that moment on, he could live a normal life. He could support himself. He could think about a family. The doors of hope burst open before him.

Peter and John had walked through that gate before. Jesus had walked by, too. But that was the day for that crippled man to walk. Today was the beginning of his day of hope. Is today your day to begin to live in hope? (Read the full story in Acts 3:1-11.)

Journey of Hope Challenge

I invite you to come on a journey with me to a place called hope. I want to change your thinking about hope. I want you to know that *hope* for a Christian isn't *hope so*. I want to change your feelings and emotions about hope because even when you are scared or doubting or discouraged, hope is real. I want to change your behavior because with the perspective of hope, you can walk with your head held high and your eyes on the world around you in confidence.

You may be wondering if this kind of hope is possible. Can you be so sure of God? Maybe you are thinking, *I've been waiting for a long time for an answer to my prayer. Where's the answer? Does God keep his promises? Is He trustworthy? Is He capable? How long must I wait? Will He ever answer?*

The answer is yes. You can hope in Jesus because with God, "waiting is not a waste of time."[7] He is faithful.

But don't take my word for it. Let's follow the evidence. All the evidence is too big for this chapter but I've picked out examples from two sources: nature and the Bible. We'll follow in the direction of the evidence and see if it leads us away from hope-so to assured hope.

Nature

When my husband George and I visited Maui, a friend arranged a trip to the top of the island's great volcano Haleakala to see the sunrise. Early that morning when we arrived at the top of the mountain, the sky was dark and the air was cold, but there were already nearly 500 people there. Each one was sitting on a hard rock wrapped in a blanket along the side of the mountain.

We joined them, found a rock, and secured our jackets and blankets around us.

Then we waited.

Though we waited for long minutes that seemed to stretch into infinity, not one person got up from their rocky perch and stomped away. No one said, "Well I guess the sun isn't coming up today!" Instead we waited.

Why? We had no signs of the sun—it was so dark we could only see right around us and the cold offered no promise of a warm sun anywhere in our future. Yet we all stayed because we had hope in the promise of the sunrise. We know the sun comes up.

Every. Day.

We placed our hope in the evidence. And we weren't disappointed. Suddenly a few rays fractured the dark eastern sky.

Then a tiny slit of the top of the circle of the sun burst over the horizon, and the bright sun ripped open the sky.

Our hope didn't rely on what we could see or feel that morning. Our hope hinged on nature, science, and history. The sun always comes up. That's the way our solar system operates. We believed it. We rooted our hope in it.

As authentic believers, we root our hope in our powerful, caring, faithful God. He never fails to show up to intervene. Even when it seems dark and cold. Even when there is no sign. He always shows up to rescue and restore.

That's the way He operates.

Believe it.

Root your hope in it.

Journey of Hope Through the Bible

During the days of Elisha, the prophet, the Arameans besieged the city of Samaria where the King of Israel resided in his palace. Imagine the city cut off from all outside supplies as the huge armies of Aram camped around the walls. My imagination sees the invaders enjoying barbecue from the campfire spits and playing card games in their tents. But in the city, people and animals were dying. Bread seemed non-existent, and food prices soared. Most people were starving. There seemed to be no hope.

The king said,

"All this misery is from the LORD! Why should I wait for the LORD any longer?" (2 Kings 6:33).

Not only had the king given up all hope of rescue, he now believed that the famine was God's fault.

Elisha countered that God would rescue the city by tomorrow.

No one believed Elisha, especially the king who gave an order to kill Elisha.

Imagine the fear.

90

Four leprous men, convinced their lives were nearly over anyway, decided to throw themselves on the mercy of the besieging army. They walked into the Aramean camp.

> "At dusk, they got up and went to the camp of
> the Arameans. When they reached the edge
> of the camp, not a man was there, for the Lord
> had caused the Arameans to hear the sound
> of chariots and horses and a great army, so
> that they said to one another, 'Look, the king
> of Israel has hired the Hittite and Egyptian
> kings to attack us!' So, they got up and fled in
> the dusk and abandoned their tents and their
> horses and donkeys. They left the camp as it
> was and ran for their lives" (2 Kings 7:5-7).

No one was there.

The king of Israel and the people of Samaria saw no hope of rescue, but they couldn't see what God was doing. They wouldn't have believed that noises in the woods would scare the mighty Aramean armies away. In their most desperate moment when nothing could set them free, God was at work.

When you feel there isn't any hope, talk to God. Ask Him what to do next. He may be at work in the camp of your enemy. That job offer may be in the next phone call. Healing may come with the next medicine that the doctor prescribes. Financial turnaround could be already in the mail.

Maybe you've been disappointed. Or betrayed. Maybe your dreams seem farther away than ever. Maybe the debt is too big; you're certain it can never be paid. Maybe the pain is so severe you're convinced you won't get through another night. I hope these pieces of evidence from the physical world and the Bible awake your soul to see the door of hope opening before you because of God's faithfulness. I want your faith to grow as you read this book so that you will be strong and sure and will grasp wide-open hope, even if the future doesn't look bright.

Novelist George Iles said, "Hope is faith holding out its hand in the dark."

The evidence is strong for a God who cares for you. Because of Him, you will not only reach out your hand in the dark but take steps in the direction of the evidence to walk in hope. If you say a situation or a person is hopeless, you are slamming the door in the face of God. Life isn't hopeless despite your situation. You don't have to curl up in a tight, closed, despairing ball. God offers you wide-open spaces where hope spreads out in every direction. He enjoys your hope,

> "The Lord delights in those who fear him, who
> put their hope in his unfailing love"
> (Psalm 174:11).

Hope is Life

Peter described our hope as living.

> "In his great mercy, he has given us new birth
> into a living hope through the resurrection of
> Jesus Christ from the dead" (1 Peter 1:3 NIV).

It sounds theological and difficult but the concept is easier to grasp than it sounds:

> "Because Jesus was raised from the dead,
> we've been given a brand-new life and have
> everything to live for"
> (1 Peter 1:3 TLB).

Understanding this concept requires us to first distinguish living hope from non-living hope. When *hope* is birthed, it is alive like a newborn child. *Hope-so* hope fades and dies with time, but hope lives. Hope is not merely surviving through loss or pain. Hope is living with joy and enthusiasm. Hope is thriving because of the loss or pain.

Peter explained that we have been granted hope. Jesus gave up everything to come to earth to live as a man.[8] On Good Friday, He suffered immense pain, was murdered in unthinkable cruelty, and was buried in a borrowed tomb.

God is never content to leave us where we are. He is always ready to take us up to the next level, to pour new wine into us.

He has plans for each of us. Fresh plans. Plans that are beyond anything we can imagine. Jeremiah recorded God's words,

> "'For I know the plans I have for you,' declares
> the Lord, 'plans to prosper you and not to harm
> you, plans to give you hope and a future'"
> (Jeremiah 29:11).

The plans that God has for us aren't simply blueprints, these plans have a purpose. Jeremiah continues,

> "Then you will call upon me and come and
> pray to me, and I will listen to you. You will
> seek me and find me when you seek me with all
> your heart. I will be found by you," declares the
> Lord...." (Jeremiah 29:12-14a).

In fact, God wants us to go to the heights beyond anything that we can dream. Habakkuk understood this when he said,

> "The Sovereign Lord is my strength; he makes
> my feet like the feet of a deer, he enables me to
> go on the heights" (Habakkuk 3:19).

God always wants to do a new thing. Isaiah recorded God's words,

"Forget the former things; do not dwell on the past. See, I am doing a new thing! Now it springs up; do you not perceive it? I am making a way in the desert and streams in the wasteland" (Isaiah 43:18-19).

This challenge is a new level of living. A new kind of aliveness. A new freedom. A new worship. A deeper relationship. A better marriage. A new home atmosphere. A better success at your job. New hope. Wide-open hope is based on God's faithfulness and His intervention. He will defeat the giant.

Chapter 8
What's a Girl to Do...

✧A Place for Reflection✧

grew up with a bit of arrogance and bluster. I could do it myself.
I didn't need God's help. I dreamed big dreams, and I was tough
enough to see them through. I believed hard work would make
the difference and if I looked good while working, no one would
see the real me or the struggles underneath.

But God had greater dreams. Bigger and more amazing than
I could ever imagine. He knew me before the womb. He put me
in my family with my father and my mother. My potential pre-
dated my parents and the messages I thought I got from them.
Yours too. If your family is dysfunctional in some way, they can't
stop God's dream or your potential. Even if you've made horrible
mistakes and failed miserably, nothing negates God's dream for
you.

Name your secret dream.

When I launched out to look good and work hard no matter what, I chose something less than God's best potential for me because I thought I could do it myself.

I didn't understand the incredible awesome truth of the love of God.

Author James Bryan Smith said, "I am one in whom Christ dwells and delights." Throughout my life, I would have fought you defending the theology of Christ dwelling in me, but I never grasped the far-fetched concept of Him delighting in me.

Do you know how much God loves you? He has magnificent dreams for you. His dreams are bigger, bolder, and more lofty than the dreams you've dreamed. He has the viewpoint of your whole life and the paths you'll take and all the people you'll meet. You can only see one little part. He never sees any limitations or excuses to keep you from the dream. Wouldn't you love to know or at least get a glimpse of the possibilities?

I believe we can discover the amazing potential of dreaming God's dream. The possibilities are endless. Most of us haven't even begun to think of the possibilities. But God is ready to show us the path.

Perhaps you are where I was on my terrible day at the city dump—at the bottom. I had no hope, and I couldn't think of any solutions. All I could think about was my mistakes and the dumb decisions I had made. On top of those miserable thoughts, for the first time in my life, I felt ill equipped and stuck. How would I continue? I didn't understand God's viewpoint was so different from mine. I could only see the lost house, the lost income, the failed me.

What happened to bring you to your lowest day of defeat?

Jacob also only thought of his trouble and his terrible situation. His story is told in Genesis 42. Jacob had 12 sons who helped in the family agricultural business. A severe famine struck the land, and there was no more food. Rumors were that Egypt had food so Jacob sent 10 of his sons to buy grain. He only sent ten because one of his sons, Joseph, was missing and presumed dead, and Jacob was afraid for the youngest son to go in case something happened to them as they traveled.

When his sons returned, they had food and a story to tell. They told their father that the governor of Egypt had spoken harshly to them and accused them of being spies. They had tried to explain that they were brothers, but the governor didn't believe them. Instead, the governor agreed to give them food for their starving families but he would keep Simeon, one of the brothers, as a security pledge. If they came back to Egypt and brought the youngest brother, the governor would know they were telling the truth, and he would release the brother who stayed in Egypt.

The old man was distraught over this arrangement. He'd already lost one son, and one son was a hostage and now they wanted to take Benjamin, the baby of the family. Jacob cried out,

"You are robbing me of my children! Joseph is gone! Simeon is gone! And now you want to take Benjamin, too. Everything is going against me!" (Genesis 42:36).

Or so he thought.

Jacob's lowest point. His place of defeat was based on what he could see and understand about the situation. But it only seemed that way. This defeat was about to lead to the greatest moment of his life. God would intervene with rescue for his family and the entire nation of Israel.

God knows the future. He sees where you are, but He also sees way beyond your place of defeat to your place of victory.

As you look back on your life, can you see a time which felt like your lowest place of defeat, but later turned out to be a place of victory?

When Josiah became King of Israel as a small boy, he inherited a terrible mess created by his father and grandfather who had set up high places to worship false gods and who did not honor or obey the one true God. Josiah made changes in the nation purging the pagan altars and images. He broke up and burned all the memorials to false gods. As we read the thirty-fourth chapter of 2 Chronicles, we breathe a sigh of relief because finally someone is seeking and following God. King Josiah hired carpenters, stone masons, and craftsmen, who worked faithfully to repair and renew the house of God. The musicians and artists restored the beauty of the temple. What a wonderful moment in the history of Israel.

As the workers were cleaning out a storeroom, some workers found the Book of the Law and when Josiah heard the words of the Book, he was broken hearted and convicted. He had been doing good and Israel was on the right track, but God had greater plans for Israel than Josiah knew until he heard the words from the Book. There would be consequences for the sins of the kings past, and Josiah understood the severity of what would happen, but it didn't stop him from pursuing God's dream. He held the best Passover ever! (2 Chronicles 35:18). The Passover was a picture of the future Messiah God would send to rescue the world. Josiah clearly understood the greater dream. He celebrated God and the plans God had for the nation.

What moment or experience has helped you see God's love for you?

Your past may include mistakes, failures, bad decisions, and terrible catastrophes, but God hasn't given up on you. You may have cleaned up your act and are doing a better job at life and at honoring God in your life, but God has even bigger plans and dreams for you. I thought I could work hard and make my life perfect. I thought if others perceived me as strong and put-together, it would be so. I made some poor choices early on, which led me down a path of more selfish desire and self enhancement. I wish I had known or could have perceived God's dream then. You may be like me—looking back at missed steps and opportunities. When Israel had nothing left and desolation encompassed them, they realized there is a God in heaven. You too can be filled with the realization of God and His love for you. You can start over today. Begin again and see what God will do. Or you may be nearer the beginning of your journey about to make decisions and leaps into life. Consider the long view, the divine view before you make a choice of necessity or whim. You can choose the best way—God's way.

Giant 3

Fear

Chapter 9
The Giant

Early one morning about 3:00 am, the phone rang. *(Something about the phone ringing in the middle of the night—you know it can't be good.)* My nephew said, "Aunt Karen! There's been an accident."

My youngest nephew, his brother, had been flown by life-flight to our city's famous trauma center. A terrible car accident had caused major injuries, especially a head wound.

We jumped out of bed to get dressed. I felt I couldn't breathe. We screamed panic prayers into the air, "Oh Lord, please no!" But our fear didn't compare to his parents (my brother and sister-in-law) who stood by the side of a country road watching the life-flight helicopter carry their youngest son away.

Fear is "a chain reaction in the brain that starts with a stressful stimulus and ends with the release of chemicals that cause a racing heart, fast breathing, and energized muscles, among other things."[9]

According to 2 Samuel 21:19, another of Goliath's brothers attacked David. This giant's name is Lahmi.[10] The giant's name means to harass or accuse.

He is the giant of fear.

Fear from sudden danger, such as falling or an accident, affects us physically. Cold hands, rapid breathing, increased heart rate, rising blood pressure, sweating, dry hands, and trembling.[11] Typically when the danger passes, we feel relief and the symptoms return to normal. Fear is also triggered artificially by scary movies because our brain identifies with the danger on screen.

Fear from emotional or mental danger, such as isolation, rejection, or other painful experiences, affects our deepest human uncertainties. "Biologically wired with a longing to belong, we fear the prospect of being cut off, demeaned, or isolated. We fear being alone. We dread change."[12]

Being alone isn't so bad. Feeling alone cuts deep into your inner being. I've felt alone in a crowded room more often than I'd like to admit. Once a year about thirty of my friends and I go away for a few days of rest and renewal, to reflect on last year and dream about the next. We laugh and hug and cry and enjoy each other. We meet with doctors and nutrition and health experts to shape our physical condition and we pray and worship and learn to strengthen our spiritual health. I love these women. Yet, sometimes in a crowded room of these treasured friends, I feel completely alone.

Sometimes I feel invisible in business meetings, at big events in huge convention centers, or in groups of a few in a quiet living room. There are people nearby, but my mind tricks me and I experience a kind of isolation. As if no one sees me or cares about me.

The loneliness of those moments is profound and desperate. If I analyze the feelings, I usually find some insecurity, *I wish I'd been more successful.* Or some grief, *I wish I hadn't done that.* Or fear, *they don't like me,* takes over.

The giant of fear can overwhelm and destroy our dreams and derail the plans of God. One fear is fear of ourselves and the decisions we made that led us to the trouble. Fear is also a product of previous pain. We shy away from the future because it too might be painful. We even fear because we doubt whether Jesus cares. The twelve disciples were in a boat with Jesus when a sudden storm frightened them. Their first reaction was to assume Jesus didn't care because he was asleep. They couldn't see beyond the storm. They were afraid.

Fear invades our space externally and internally.

External Fear

Fear caused externally happens when sudden changes seem overpowering. A car pulls in front of yours. You walk down a dark unfamiliar path. You slip on stairs or see a child run for a busy street. Places, people, situations, and words strike fear—even the weather.

Around 4 in the morning, the alerts sounded on our phones warning us of strong storms in the area. My husband turned on the TV, and we watched the radar. The weather guy said the storms were lining up one after the other in a "train" effect and following the same path—over our neighborhood.

There were circular cells in the storms indicating a tornado could form. Our Great Pyrenees was already in the tub—so frightened by the thunder. The weather guy said the worst storm would be over a nearby air field at 5:23 AM. Since the air field is close, I said, "It's 5:21 so it must be over us now." At that moment, we heard the sound! (If you've ever wondered if you would recognize the sound of a tornado—believe me, it is a sound you've never heard before. You will know.)

We ran to the bathtub and climbed in with the dog...me over her. George over me. And then it struck. House shaking, sounds of shattered glass as the windows broke, the whistling sounds of the winds whipping the roof, the trees and fences, and houses.

All the while, George and I were praying, screaming to Jesus as loud as our voices would raise.

The fear was intense as doom loomed over us.

And then it was totally quiet. And still. Quietness like I never heard before.

And dark.

We stepped out of the bathroom and glass crunched beneath our feet. The window over our bed was broken and the glass was blown all the way to the opposite wall and down the hall. The wind had stripped the sheets off the bed. *So, glad we didn't stay there.*

When daylight finally arrived, we saw the devastation. Every fence down. Trees snapped into shreds. The front porch pillars down and bent. Windows smashed. Big sections of roof…gone. Trees in the swimming pool. Sheds torn apart and our backyard neighbor's shed upside down. So many tree branches covering the front porch, it looked like a jungle—no light could come through. Furniture tossed around like toys. Glass table top on the outdoor furniture shattered. Neighbor's gazebo in our yard. And so much more.

But the damage was nothing compared to the fear in that bathtub. According to *Psychology Today*, fear is a vital response to physical and emotional danger. If we didn't feel it, we couldn't protect ourselves from legitimate threats.[13] But if we respond to all situations no matter how minor as if they were life-threatening, we have allowed fear to reign and control us.

Some fears grow out of phobias. Virtually any social situation or object can become a phobia. Fear of heights, fear of spiders, fear of dogs, the phobia lists are endless and are usually exhibited by anxiety. Doctors explain the difference between fear and anxiety, "Fear is the emotional response to real or perceived imminent threat, whereas anxiety is anticipation of future threat."

(real or imagined)

The giant of fear attacks us in the present with sudden threats and in the future with potential hazards.

Internal Fear

Fear is not always because of impending danger. The giant attacks us internally in our minds and spirits. The giant Lahmi's shouting would have sounded like this.

"You are weak."

"You missed the boat."

"You did it again."

"You will fall flat."

"You can't do it."

"You won't ever amount to anything."

He shouts at us and fuels our internal fear.

I have known the Lord since my childhood so my heart is conditioned and quick to believe that God loves me and that He is faithful. I believe He will intervene in my situations and snatch me from the jaws of defeat. Especially when the discouragement or defeat is out of my control or heaped on me by some other person's decision or mistake.

But I don't find it as easy to believe I will be rescued when my problems are caused by my mistakes or my disobedience. Is God faithful when I'm unfaithful? Does God swoop in to intervene and rescue me when I deserve the pain I'm facing? My questions lead to fear.

The giant of fear shows up often. For me the fear has its roots in the idea that I have caused the problem by some stupid decision or by words that came flying out of my mouth before I thought how they would sound. Fear that I will be seen as a failure not as a success. Fear that no one will like me because I talk too much or embellished a story or wasn't attentive to details. Fear looms over me taunting and mocking, harassing and tormenting. *You act like all is well, but if they knew the truth. Your heart is bitter but you keep smiling…someone will see through you. Your laugh is a little too loud and high pitched to be believable. Yeah, you look good but if they could see behind the façade, they would never bother with you. Not one of these people is a real friend even though they act friendly.*

I have a chart in my mind. On that chart, I check off my mistakes.

You did it again- Check.
Exaggeration – Check.
Harsh words – Check.
Mean thoughts – Check.
Failure to trust God – Check.
Missed chance to witness – Check.
Money shouldn't have spent – Check.
The phone call I didn't make – Check.

We must fight the giant of fear because we can't let fear make our decisions. Anup Kochar said, "A fear of weakness only strengthens the weakness and produces conformity."

Chapter 10
The Weapon

When Lahmi showed up shouting, "Be afraid. Be very afraid," one of David's men stood to fight and slay the giant. His name was Elhanan.

Elhanan's name means the mercy of God.

God is full of mercy.

Mercy conquers fear.

The usual definition of mercy is compassion and kindness shown toward someone whom you have the power or right to punish. In relation to God, the definition expands, "love that responds to human need in an unexpected or unmerited way."[15]

Author David Mathis wrote, "The mercy of God is one of the most precious realities in the world, one of the most revealing themes in all the Bible, and one of the most tragically misunderstood truths about God. If you want to know who God is, if you want to peek into his heart, it is not the display of his just wrath and cosmic power to which you should look. Rather, set your eye on his mercy, without minimizing the fullness of his might, and take in the life-changing panorama."[16]

The kind of mercy that God has for us is hard to understand for several reasons. One reason is because humans tend to be retaliatory. We want revenge. *I'll get them for that!* We are also quick to criticize and judge when others have failed. Be honest. What do you think when you see someone grossly overweight or living under a bridge? Our mercy meter is weak.

God sees *all* about each of us, and He knows we are sinners.

"For everyone has sinned; we all fall short of God's glorious standard" (Romans 3:23-24).

And yet He sends mercy.

When I fail—even if I've made the worst choice or said the most horrible words—He says, "I know, I know. It's okay. I love you." He offers mercy.

Re-read the definition. Mercy is compassion toward someone you have the right to crush. But God's mercy is more than human mercy—He offers unexpected and unmerited love. I don't deserve mercy and I'm surprised and astonished and humbled by it.

God conquers our fear with His mercy toward us. We come to the end of ourselves and our ability to cope, but He extends our abilities and our path by giving mercy.

Faith is the key to relying on His mercy. Author Max Lucado said, "Feed your fears and your faith will starve. Feed your faith and your fears will starve."

The chain reaction of fear was active in all of us that night of my nephew's accident. At the hospital, we huddled in fear. We prayed, asking for healing, and we prayed for the doctor's skills and sure hands.

Many hours later, we got the good news that my nephew would be okay; we wept with joy and relief.

I asked my brother how he handled the stress and fear. He said, "I went to the hospital chapel and begged God to take me, not my son. Then I asked for mercy. Faith got me through. Mercy saved my son."

God knows our guilt, yet He is delighted to show mercy to us.

"Where is another God like you, who pardons the guilt of the remnant, overlooking the sins of his special people? You will not stay angry with your people forever, because you delight in showing unfailing love" (Micah 7:18).

NKJV = "mercy"

"He delights in"

"be mercy"

You may not be able to see God's mercy in your situation. You can't point to a healing or a good test result or a reconciliation or a financial miracle. I hear your cry. I don't have the total answer. But one truth I know: God is more inclined to mercy than wrath. He is not part mercy; He is everything mercy could ever hope to be. Build your life on the mercies of God. Cling to God's mercy. Mercy is His heart. Leave the results in His hand.

When fear
destroys...

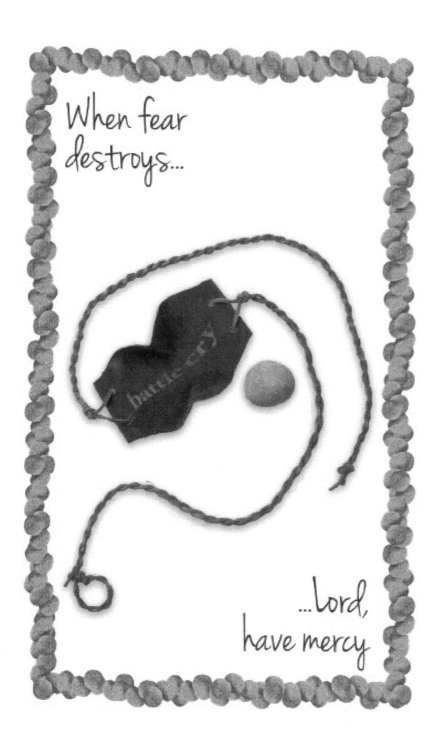

...Lord,
have mercy

Chapter 11
Fight for Your Life

Whose voice will I heed?

When a woman looks into the mirror and finds wrinkles and features she doesn't like, she has to face the facts of life: she's older; she's not the same; she sags; she bulges. Women can choose a healthy lifestyle and discover brightness mentally, emotionally, and spiritually even if it feels like the lights have gone out. The choices depend on the voice we hear.

Self-talk and self-condemnation are the enemy's most successful tools, but God's Word reveals the enemy's lies and shows the truth of who we are in Christ. As author Mary Anne Radmacher said, "Sometimes courage is the quiet voice at the end of the day saying, 'I will try again tomorrow.'"

When we try to be positive and do good for our self, the results end in another reason to hear our negative voice. For example, eating healthy. We punish ourselves by restricting every bite and never enjoying the bounty of lovely, rich, delicious delights around us, or we overindulge and eat too many sweets and fats. Either way is destructive. If we over restrict our food, we feel deprived. If we overeat, we feel shame.

Another example is negativity. We scold ourselves when we try anything new, assuming we are going to fail. Some people are so negative they can't buy a new car for fear some of the new gadgets will break. These same people are never for making changes in organizations or trying new ways to advance the message of the Gospel.

Our inner voice shows up in attitudes such as deference to everyone else and becoming the perpetual victim, never standing for ourself. Or we overspend on items that make us feel good or that we think will make us feel good.

Friendships are sabotaged by our inner voices as we imagine that a person couldn't possibly like us. Our internal voice fuels overeating, drug and alcohol abuse, obsession with possessions, or compulsive shopping. Whose voice do you hear?

Beating Rejection

My critical inner voice took over recently when I faced rejection. A friend—a dear, close friend—wounded me with her words and her actions. Wounds from a friend are unexpected and especially painful because your love for the friend is deflated like a punctured balloon. It is hard to know where to turn and who you can trust. You second guess yourself. *What did I do to cause this to happen?* And you feel a deep sadness driven by anger. *How could she be so mean? I miss my friend. I don't deserve it.*

And then, our personal faultfinder begins to work overtime. *She not only did this to you, she is talking about you to other people. She hates you. Remember when she….*

My emotional pain was visceral and grew into a gloomy circle.

During this time of pain, our church held a 3-night prayer meeting. The prayer service began with worship music and powerful encouragement from the pulpit. And the congregation prayed. Aloud. Everyone praying at the same time is part of our church culture and is a beautiful expression of communication with the Father. But I will admit that the cacophony of noises distracts me. Part of the reason for feeling uncomfortable is my socializer personality. *I want to hear what each person is saying.* I'm easily sidetracked. Part of the reason for my distraction is that I grew up in a quiet church atmosphere, and this way to worship is unusual to me. But I've learned to love the prayers of the people around me even though it feels different.

That night, I was desperate to reach out to the Father because of my personal pain, so I focused, closing my eyes to shut out the distractions around me. As I closed my eyes, I noticed that the lights from the stage area were still shining through my eyelids. You've probably experienced this phenomenon, too. The eye still holds the images you last saw even though the lids are closed. I didn't think anything unusual about seeing the dim lights through my eyelids. Because I didn't know what to pray, I repeated a one-word prayer, "Jesus. Jesus. Jesus."

And then something strange happened. I felt a cold dark shadow and the light in my eyelids went completely black. The sensation scared me. I quickly opened my eyes and stared at the front of the auditorium. Deep within I sensed that this darkness was vile. I closed my eyes again and prayed louder, "Jesus!" The dark shadow returned. Somehow I knew this darkness was the spirit of rejection and that if I gave in, I would fall deeper into the fear and pain of it. I prayed, "Lord, I don't understand this darkness. I sense it is evil. I ask you to take it away and destroy any power the spirit of rejection may have over me."

In that moment, I felt relief from my pain. Fear left me. Darkness and rejection flew away. The giant of fear fell. I sensed the peace and joy of the Lord and in my heart, I heard His gentle sweet voice,

"Don't be afraid, for I am with you. Don't
be discouraged, for I am your God. I will
strengthen you and help you. I will hold you up
with my victorious right hand"
(Isaiah 41:10 NLT).

My experience wasn't about my friend. It was a giant attack.
I could choose to hear the giant whisper, *you are all alone.* Or I
could choose hope and then cling to God's mercy. Slaying the
giant depended on the voice I heeded.

Too often the giant only has one voice in my life—mine. I
speak or think the words of rejection and condemnation into my
mind and spirit. I give voice to the vengeance, which says hate
or hurt her back. My voice becomes one with the giant's voice.

Or I can listen to the voice of God which says, "Mercy."

Chapter 12
What's a Girl to Do...

✧A Place for Reflection✧

sabelle is a wimp! One crack of thunder and she hides in a closet or tub. Any loud noise like a helicopter or jet plane or loud truck and she runs for cover, frightened and worried. She's a beautiful girl, but she is a total wimp. She is a Great Pyrenees.

One foggy morning, I let Isabelle out the back door. She typically returns fast because she is afraid of noises and the dark, but on this day, she didn't come.

Then I saw her—in the swimming pool. And I saw fear.

Somehow, she had fallen in and now she was clinging to the side of the pool with her paws digging into the concrete. I ran to her because I know how terrified she is of water.

As I looked down at her, I noticed that her back feet were one inch from the steps on the deep end. One move of her legs, and she could find the platform. I tried to get her to swing one foot over a bit so she could push herself out of the pool. She wouldn't budge.

I considered prying her front paws from the edge of the pool, forcing her into the water because we have taught her to swim and to turn toward the steps in the shallow end of the pool. She's not a great swimmer, but she knows to paddle to the other steps nearby.

Instead I took pity on her. I reached down and lifted her out of the pool.

If Isabelle would have moved one of her back legs an inch or so, she would have been able to get the footing necessary to push herself out of the pool. The answer to our fear is often nearby too. If we will look around us, we might find the answer and raise ourselves out of our trouble.

What answers do you see nearby that might relieve your fear?

Isabelle knows how to swim. We taught her and worked with her long enough so she could always turn around to find the big steps. Sometimes when you and I are fearful, we can gain courage by drawing on the skills, expertise, and talents within us. All we need to do is calm down and move in the direction of our training to get to safety.

What skills do you possess that can help you with the emotion of fear?

But that morning I had mercy on Isabelle and reached down, placing my strong arms beneath her and lifted her out. Often when we are in trouble, God has mercy on us as frail human beings.

"He reached down from on high and took hold
of me; he drew me out of deep waters"
(Psalm 18:16 NIV).

Write a prayer asking God for mercy when you are fearful.

When fear strikes, look around to find a way to push yourself out or swim to safety using the skills you have already acquired. Or cry out to God for mercy and He will rescue you. But don't be a wimp!

Giant 4

Self

Chapter 13
The Giant

One more brother tried to kill David. He has no name but he has unusual features.

> "In another battle with the Philistines at Gath, they encountered a huge man with six fingers on each hand and six toes on each foot, twenty-four in all, who was also a descendant of the giants" (2 Samuel 21:20).

Through some misstep of his DNA, he grew six fingers on each hand and six toes on each foot. Imagine the taunts of his childhood as the neighborhood children called him names and laughed at his hands and feet. Imagine how self-focused and self-centered his life. *Why do I have to look this way? What's wrong with me? Why aren't I like the others?* The self-conscious feelings of being the center of attention for all the wrong reasons.

And as if nature wasn't satisfied to give him too many digits, he grew taller and bigger than all the other kids eventually becoming a giant. I feel a bit sorry for "no name," and I'm not surprised that he took the path to violence and anger.

During the battle at Gath, I imagine he screamed words like, "I am the biggest meanest dude you've ever encountered." And shouted, "I will succeed where my brothers failed. Because it is all about me, and I am the winner." I can see him standing straight, shoulders raised shouting, "I am god."

He is the giant of self.

In the Bible, six is the number of man, and when you see the number six you can be sure man is looking out for himself. Self-seeking. Self-exalting. Self-assurance. Self-pleasure.

Even if we hate ourselves, our self-hate focuses on self. And self-esteem, which seems to be a good trait, becomes a giant because "it is all about me."

Self is our biggest problem. One mentor suggested we put a sign on the mirror, "You're looking at the problem." We like ourselves more than anyone else. We will do whatever is necessary to protect and promote ourselves. In the corporate world, owners and management and individual employees are looking out for themselves. In culture, we hear, "Let me do my thing." Or "What I do hurts no one else so leave me alone." Or "I'll find my own way I don't need God."

Even in Christian circles, we ask God for leadership and then we take control from Him so we "can do it our way."

Self is why we don't read the Bible and pray regularly. Caring about self keeps us from helping and serving others. Self is why we don't confess our sin. Self is why we let our worries grow into fear.

The Psalmist said,

"I am fearfully and wonderfully made"
(Psalm 139:10).

Humans are wondrous creatures. We need only to look at one small part of the human body to be filled with awe about the complexity and wonder. Consider the human hand. Twenty-seven bones, 29 joints, and at least 123 ligaments, fingers with unique fingerprints, and opposing thumbs make the hand complex and incredible. Ponder the human eye, complicated and beautiful, the eye allows us to perceive and understand the world around us. We have 100,000 miles of blood vessels, a 23-foot-long small intestine, a complex heart, a computer brain, and intricate body systems.

No wonder we like ourselves so much. We pamper and indulge ourselves. We inflate our self-opinion with excessive self-importance and overestimate our good features while underestimating our weaknesses. We make important decisions often based on how it will affect us.

Emotionally and socially, egotism hampers our ability to get along with others. But "self" impedes us spiritually more than any other area. Self-esteem sounds like a positive and helpful concept. And the idea is accurate to an extent because we shouldn't hate ourselves. However, when we are focused on ourselves solely, we lose our focus on Jesus. We become ruled by the flesh instead of the spirit. Author Jennifer Kennedy Dean calls it, "flimflam flesh." She says, "The flesh is more than the body...all sin has flesh as its starting point."[17]

Let's consider the various perspectives on self.

In Christianity, the *self* is often viewed negatively as the reason for our failures and sins. Part of this view is based on the words of Jeremiah.

"The human heart is the most deceitful of all things, and desperately wicked. Who really knows how bad it is?" (Jeremiah 17:9).

It is our nature to rebel against God and promote self as Paul warned, [men will be] "lovers of self...rather than lovers of God" (2 Timothy 3:2,4).

127

Psychology is often focused on loving self, esteeming self, and finding self-fulfillment. Unfortunately, much of self-love thinking has developed into participation trophies, which as the *New York Times* points out are "handed out like party favors" and are a "potentially dangerous life message to children."[18]

For believers, the challenge is finding a balance between knowing our propensity for sin and recognizing that we are created in God's image. This balance is found in God's grace.

"But God showed his great love for us by sending Christ to die for us while we were still sinners" (Romans 5:8).

Paul fought the battle with self. Read this passage from his letter to the Romans. It is a long passage but it will help us understand the war with self.

"The trouble is with me, for I am all too human, a slave to sin. I don't really understand myself, for I want to do what is right, but I don't do it. Instead, I do what I hate. But if I know that what I am doing is wrong, this shows that I agree that the law is good. So, I am not the one doing wrong; it is sin living in me that does it. And I know that nothing good lives in me, that is, in my sinful nature. I want to do what is right, but I can't. I want to do what is good, but I don't. I don't want to do what is wrong, but I do it anyway. But if I do what I don't want to do, I am not really the one doing wrong; it is sin living in me that does it. I have discovered this principle of life—that when I want to do what is right, I inevitably do what is wrong. I love God's law with all my heart. But there is another power within me that is at war with my mind. This power makes me a slave to the sin that is still within me. Oh, what a miserable person I am! Who will free me from this life that is dominated by sin and death? Thank God! The answer is in Jesus Christ our Lord. So, you see how it is: In my mind, I really want to obey God's law, but because of my sinful nature I am a slave to sin" (Romans 7:14-25).

The battle with self requires the endurance of a warrior and the strength of our God.

Chapter 14
The Weapon

The giant of self is much too big and much too powerful to face alone. We need weapons.

The mighty warrior Jonathan killed the giant of no name with 12 fingers and 12 toes. Jonathan means given by God, God has given us all the weapons we need to fight the battle with self.

His Word

Not only is the Bible the all-time best seller, it is the most important book ever written. The Bible contains history, poetry, literature, morality codes, redemption, and much more. People have died for the Bible, and it is used as a guide for countless lives. Centuries of critical skeptics have never found any inaccuracies. Millions of lives have been changed, redeemed, and freed by reading and believing the matchless story of God's love for humankind.

Isaiah wrote about the longevity and permanence of the Word,

"The rain and snow come down from the
heavens and stay on the ground to water the

earth. They cause the grain to grow, producing seed for the farmer and bread for the hungry. It is the same with my word. I send it out, and it always produces fruit. It will accomplish all I want it to, and it will prosper everywhere I send it" (Isaiah 55:10-11).

The author of Hebrews wrote about the power of the Word,

"For the word of God is alive and powerful. It is sharper than the sharpest two-edged sword, cutting between soul and spirit, between joint and marrow. It exposes our innermost thoughts and desires" (Hebrews 4:12).

The Word is to be read aloud, explained and preached, searched, and followed. With this grandest of gifts, our Father has shown us how to defeat the giant of self.

- ✦ Lay aside the old self. Ephesians 4:22-23
- ✦ Christ lives in me. Galatians 2:20
- ✦ Deny self and take up my cross. Luke 9:23-24

Also see Romans 6:11-14; 12:1-1-2; 1 Peter 4:1-2.

Prayer

Prayer is a unique gift because it allows mere humans to speak to the Creator of the universe. The Bible tells us to ask and keep on asking, to seek and keep on seeking, to knock and keep on knocking.

"Keep on asking, and you will receive what you ask for. Keep on seeking, and you will find. Keep on knocking, and the door will be opened to you" (Matthew 7:7).

God is greater than any feelings of self-importance and greater than any feelings of self-pity you may experience. Life is hard, and we naturally protect ourselves first by retreating or by lashing out. Prayer will help us learn to trust God in the tough times. Lifting my voice in prayer acknowledges that God is the superior power and leads me to trust Him instead of myself.

The beauty of communicating with God through prayer is that we begin to understand His heart and trust Him instead of self.

Listening

Beloved author Oswald Chambers said, "We don't consciously and deliberately disobey God—we simply don't listen to Him."[19] If you want to defeat the giant of self, listening to God may be your best weapon. Hearing God's voice raises suspicious alarms with some people. *Do you hear voices? Do you hear His voice audibly? How does He sound? Why haven't I ever heard Him speak?* I often caution professional speakers whom I am coaching to be careful about saying phrases such as "God said...." or "God told me..." because the phrases are misunderstood by hearers who fasten on to the idea of God speaking audibly and never hear the rest of the presentation.

Listening to God is a deliberate choice to shut out the chaos around you and focus your thoughts.[20] God speaks through His Word when a verse you may have read many times before affects you in a new way. This fresh understanding of a passage is the direct work of the Holy Spirit who converts the words into instruments of power for you. God connects to you through circumstances when you see Him answer a prayer or intervene in a situation. God speaks to you through others who are courageous enough to speak truth in love.

Augustine, who lived AD 354-430, said, "God wants to give us something but cannot because our hands are full." To slay the giant of self, we must ask, "Is my hand ready to receive or is it clutched around something that I refuse to let go?" Opening your hand to receive the gifts of God requires a change of heart and motive. Attitudes like *I deserve this* or *I earned it* will close your fist tightly, preventing His gifts from impacting your life and feeding the selfishness within. Reading the Word will seem like empty letters on a page; prayer will feel like noise in the room; listening will be pointless; thankfulness and friendship will fade into the background. But a heart ready to receive will find comfort, peace, joy, and courage in these gifts.

Author C.S. Lewis said, "Out of ourselves, into Christ, we must go. The more we get what we now call 'ourselves' out of the way and let Him take us over, the more truly ourselves we become."[21]

I believe we are consumed with self because we don't understand the magnitude of our God. We think of Him in human terms, putting human boundaries and weaknesses into our image of Him. We limit Him with our humanity. God neither thinks nor acts the way we would. To defeat self, we must not look at God through our finite eyes for He is a super natural God.

One event told in the New Testament explains how killing the giant of self will change our life forever—the story of Lazarus.

****

She sat on the mat exhausted and emptied. There were no more tears. Now she felt dead—like her brother lying in the grave at the edge of town. She had paced. She had thumped her fingers on the walls in a frantic attempt to keep him from dying, but she had no powers to save him. She tried the poultices and even resorted to the hated leaches but he continued to get worse and then he died. Now four days later, all her energy and influence spent, she stared into the dark room.

"Martha, Martha," she could hear the women before they came to her door. "He's here. Jesus is here."

"Hummph." She sighed, "too late." She bolted out the door into the courtyard. When she saw his familiar gait among the group on the road, a roughness pushed its way into her throat. "If you had been here, he would not have died."

The crowd gasped and silence fell over the crowd but Jesus smiled and touched her hand. "If you believe, you will see the glory of God."

Then Jesus called out to the cave, "Lazarus, come out." The silent awestruck crowd saw Lazarus come walking. Once dead, now he was clearly alive.

****

In this familiar story of Lazarus' resurrection we celebrate God's mighty powerful hand. We recognize and identify his ultimate power over life and death. The story offers hope for a future resurrection for us. We delight to see that Jesus cared so much for His friends that He came at the time of deepest sorrow.

As often as I have read this passage and as often as I have heard sermons and teachings on it (and even taught it myself) I haven't paid attention to the (as Paul Harvey said) rest of the story. What happened to Lazarus after that day? Did he go back to his life in Bethany? Did he begin a ministry telling his life's story to crowds in the region? What became of him?

Immediately a Bethany revival emerged.

"Therefore, many of the Jews who had come to visit Mary, and had seen what Jesus did, put their faith in him" (John 11:45).

135

For the mourners who came to the wake, Jesus' miracle triggered belief.

But some were not amazed or astonished. They reported the incident to the authorities in Jerusalem.

"But some of them went to the Pharisees and told them what Jesus had done" (John 11:46).

The news of Lazarus' resurrection caused a stir and an emergency meeting of the Sanhedrin.

"If we let him go on like this, everyone will believe in him, and then the Romans will come and take away both our place and our nation" (John 11:48).

Threatened by loss of power, they began at that moment a plot to kill Jesus.

Jesus left town for a while, but what about Lazarus? He had been accepted by the Jews before. His friendship with Jesus was never questioned before. His status in society was not a threat until he became a first-person witness of the resurrection power of Jesus. If anyone was an eyewitness, Lazarus was. The crowds came to see him. To hear him tell of hearing Jesus' voice while he lay in the tomb. How he felt his lifeless limbs begin to move. How he once again breathed air. How he stumbled out following the voice of the Master. The crowds couldn't get enough of it. Even when Jesus returned for Passover, people crushed in on Lazarus to once again see the miracle.

"Meanwhile a large crowd of Jews found out that Jesus was there and came, not only because of him but also to see Lazarus, whom he had raised from the dead" (John 12:9).

News of Lazarus spread over the valleys toward Jerusalem and more and more people believed.

"For on account of him many of the Jews were going over to Jesus and putting their faith in him" (John 12:10).

So many people believed that the religious leaders plotted to kill Lazarus, too.

Finally on Palm Sunday, when Jesus entered the city on a donkey, the crowds shouted "Hosanna, Glory to God" primarily because of the miracle of Lazarus' resurrection.

"Now the crowd that was with him when he called Lazarus from the tomb and raised him from the dead continued to spread the word. Many people, because they had heard that he had given this miraculous sign, went out to meet him" (John 12:17-18).

Why was Lazarus causing the world to turn to Jesus? Because he had died. As awkward as it sounds, winning the battle over self requires dying first. Dying becomes living. Dying becomes life.

Jesus explained it as he warned the disciples about the coming crucifixion.

"The hour has come for the Son of Man to be glorified. I tell you the truth, unless a kernel of wheat falls to the ground and dies, it remains only a single seed. But if it dies, it produces many seeds. The man who loves his life will lose it, while the man who hates his life in this world will keep it for eternal life. Whoever

serves me must follow me; and where I am, my
servant also will be. My Father will honor the
one who serves me" (John 12:23-26).

We must die before we can live. As long as I am full of
concern about me—whether I'll get the promotion or will my
friends invite me to the party. As long as I want what's easy for
me or what is pleasant for me, I will never focus truly on Jesus.
But the decision to focus on Jesus is not meant to put me into the
background. It is to kill me. To get rid completely, once and for
all, died and buried, all those little self-nuances that haunt me.

Jesus loved Lazarus too much to heal him when illness
threatened his life. Jesus loved Lazarus so much that he allowed
him to die.

It may be what David meant when he said,

You O Lord keep my lamp burning. You turn
my darkness into light" (Psalm 18:27b).

In my darkness, I find light in Jesus. In my utter despair and
the killing of me, I find life in Him.

Until you have given up yourself to Him, you will not have
a real self.[22]

When self
rises up...

...faith is
the victory

Chapter 15
Fight for Your Life

Will I allow God to use my past as His launchpad for my future?

"Give me your lantern and compass, give me
a map. So, I can find my way to your holy hill,
to the place of your presence, to the place of
worship" (Psalm 43:3).

As a child, I often went to my grandmother's country home.
There, I was free to roam the nearby fields, pastures, and woods.
No longer hemmed in by the fears of city streets. What freedom!
Out in the fields, I could be anything. I danced like a ballerina,
twirled my baton like a pro, and promenaded like a princess.
What potential! I sang to the top of my voice and even preached a
few sermons to the cattle. What ability! At the edge of the woods,
my brother built a play town complete with roads and bridges. In
that make-believe world, I was the president. What power!

When I became a Christian, I experienced those same
emotions on a deeper level because Jesus gave me freedom from
the guilt and misery of my flaws and sins. Trusting Him opened
the possibility that I could do anything. Depending on Him

provided the skills and abilities that I didn't possess on my own. He filled me with power and strength.

Prior to knowing Jesus, our lives are chaos—weak and failing. But when we discover the salvation of Jesus, we become a new person. Paul said,

> "Therefore, if anyone is in Christ, he is a new creation; the old has gone, the new has come!" (2 Corinthians 5:17-18 NIV).

What does it mean to be a new creature?

> "Do not conform any longer to the pattern of this world but be transformed by renewing of your mind. Then you will be able to test and approve what God's will is – his good, pleasing and perfect will" (Romans 12:2 NIV).

The English word "transformed" is translated from the Greek word *metamorphoo* or metamorphosis. Remember that word from seventh-grade biology? Metamorphosis means change. God longs for us to change into new creatures.

Grasshoppers

In my grandmother's fields, there were thousands of grasshoppers—large, small, brown, white, and green. As I walked through the tall grass, they led the way. At first, I assumed that the small ones were babies and the large were adults, but I learned that the tiniest creature could have been the oldest adult.

Some of us are like the grasshopper. We are older but we are not much different than when we were novice believers. We have grown up, but we have not grown. We are leaders yet we display childish attributes: envy, selfishness, and pride. These attitudes disguise themselves as concern for the purity of the church or doctrine. They show up in business-meeting arguments or whispered complaints about the pastor, the music, or the carpet color.

We look like a grown up but we haven't absorbed the nutrition of Bible study, the encouragement of prayer, or the rest of meditation. Without them, we never grow up. We look like adult Christians, but we are actually big babies.

Bullfrogs

Many of us make changes like the tadpole. Born with gills and fins, he swims in the water. When he morphs, he loses the tail, develops lungs, and grows strong legs. He hops out of the water and breathes air. Once quiet, he now has a voice. Once water-bound, he is free. Completely changed.

Some of us have also changed. Our old language vanished. We dislike the old parties with the old friends. We walk and talk a new way. Our old desires have morphed.

But the frog continues to live around the pond. He sits on the lily pads and occasionally jumps into the water for a swim. He is changed. Yet he clings to the old life. A Christian who behaves like a bullfrog also dabbles in his old ways. He watches the same TV programs, reads the same books, and goes the same places. True metamorphosis, requires change and separation. There is no freedom in a dual life.

Butterflies

What could be more beautiful than a colorful butterfly flitting from flower to flower? The brilliant, feather-like wings and the grace of flight both amaze and fascinate us.

Transformed Christians are like the caterpillar that enters the chrysalis and emerges as a colorful butterfly. No longer a brown worm inching its way along the ground, the butterfly experiences all the beauty and freedom of flight.

God intends for us to fly free too. As the butterfly defies gravity to soar, so God longs to see us reach heights that we have never experienced before. In fact, His greatest desire for us is that we would become like Him. Paul called it being transformed into the likeness of Christ.

> "And we, who with unveiled faces all reflect
> the Lord's glory, are being transformed into
> his likeness with ever-increasing glory, which
> comes from the Lord, who is the Spirit."
> (2 Corinthians 3:18 NIV).

Perhaps you already know that God wants you to be a butterfly using all the talents, abilities, and personality that He has given you. Like many believers, you want to be all that you can be in Him. You know that you have failed and haven't lived up to your potential. As you read about grasshoppers and bullfrogs, you see yourself.

But God gives second chances. At the moment of salvation, God allowed us to take a new slate and begin again. Since then, even when we fail, God isn't shocked by our mistakes or by our rebellion. He says, "Make a U-turn. Try again."

Starting over feels good. A child in an art class loves to be given a new piece of art paper to start the project over. As adults, we love a New Year, a new car, or a new house—or a new purse. We love to start over and try again. God forgives and forgets our mistakes. He is not only the God of second chances; he gives third, fourth, hundredth, and thousandth chances, too.

The Potter Principle

Jeremiah observed the potter at work. His observations give us a glimpse of how God works in us.

> "So, I went down to the potter's house, and I
> saw him working at the wheel. But the pot he
> was shaping from the clay was marred in his

hands; so the potter formed it into another pot, shaping it as seemed best to him" (Jeremiah 18:2-4 NIV)

A potter spends hours and days working on the clay. He molds and stretches it. He tears it apart and presses it together again. He removes the lumps and He may work for hours or put it on a shelf for a while. But when the clay is ready, workable, and pliable, the potter transforms it from a lump of clay to a beautiful useful pitcher or bowl.

Paid in Full

Jesus paid the price for our sins to free us from the destruction we deserved. No amount of discussion could explain, expound, or understand the magnitude of His sacrifice for us. Paul mentioned it in his letter to the Philippians when he listed the downward steps that Jesus took when he came to earth.

"Who, being in very nature God, did not consider equality with God something to be grasped, but made himself nothing, taking the very nature of a servant, being made in human likeness. And being found in appearance as a man, he humbled himself and became obedient to death—even death on a cross" (Philippians 2:6-8 NIV).

This act of humility on the part of the king of the universe saved us. Yet that was not all. Jesus said,

"I am come that you might have life and have it to the full" (John 10:10b NIV).

He came so that we could not only have life but that we could also enjoy life. He offers us life in abundance. He promises life in him to be better than anything we ever dreamed. His is an overflowing life. A successful life. A higher life. It is the only true Christian life.

Sold Out

An event in a stadium or arena is not sold out unless a ticket for every seat has been purchased. It doesn't matter that thousands and thousands of tickets are sold; if one seat on the back row in the farthest corner is vacant, the event is not a sellout. Being sold out to God is only possible when all the details of our lives are under His control. Not one thing, no matter how small, can be held back. Paul said that compared to knowing Jesus, all else is trash.

> "What is more, I consider everything a loss compared to the surpassing greatness of knowing Christ Jesus my Lord, for whose sake I have lost all things. I consider them rubbish, that I may gain Christ" (Philippians 3:8 NIV).

Is There More?

The Christian life is a bit like mountain climbing. Maybe as you read these words you think, *Mountain climbing? Me? Mountain living maybe. Ah yes, the view from the top. Miles and miles of beauty before my eyes. Peacefully enjoying the panoramas and vistas. Snow in the winter. Wildflowers and critters in the summer. Yes, mountain top living is for me, but climbing—no thanks.*

Perhaps you feel lost in the valley of busyness and compromise. Tangled in the weeds of bad habits, selfish attitudes, and hurt feelings with not much time lately to gaze at the mountain, let alone plan a trip to the top. Besides you've tried climbing before and failed. Every step was slippery; dangerous precipices

146

loomed. Finding a handhold was tricky. Maybe mountain climbing isn't for you.

Yet, something calls me—something says, "There's more to life than this valley." More than the everyday chores of life. More than shuffling papers and pushing computer keys. More than constant financial worries. More than the loneliness that we sometimes feel in a crowd.

Jesus calls us to climb. We may hit bumps and get bruised. We may need Band-Aids. But we're not climbing for the climb but for the joy of the higher ground—for the opportunity to honor Him.

"For I fully expect and hope that I will never be ashamed, but that I will continue to be bold for Christ, as I have been in the past. And I trust that my life will bring honor to Christ, whether I live or die (Philippians 1:20)- 21

Chapter 16
What's a Girl to Do...

✧A Place for Reflection✧

God built me with a lot of confidence, assurance, and ambition. And the events of my life reinforced all those characteristics. Confidence that I could do it. Assurance that if I worked hard, I could have it all. Ambition to want the best and the most. But how easily I forget Him and His contribution to my life and His gifts. To say I was self-sufficient is the understatement of the year.

I'll Drive

My daddy's hands mystified me. Big. Huge. Rough. In fact, one hand could cover my entire forearm with sandpaper bigness. One finger, broken or jammed in some rough-necking job somewhere, never bent completely when he closed his fist. The one finger mesmerized me and every time I think of him, I see those hands and that finger.

When I was ten, Daddy and I were at the old barn on the country family homestead. I chased feral cats and played all the parts of a play I'd invented on the spot. Inside the barn, he slammed around the junk; muttering, "Where did I put those jars?"

His thrashing around comforted me with a peculiar security. *If he can't find stuff, then life is normal.* No one would ever quit our family because "we still gotta get something cleaned up or organized." In an odd way, his pack-rat tendencies reassured and offered sanctuary, and yet his powerful personality scared the socks off me, especially if I ever got in his way.

I found a stage of sorts in the far reaches of the barn. I sang my rendition of Maria's "I Feel Pretty" from *West Side Story*, my all-time favorite musical, and while I was pretending and singing, I heard a scream.

"Daddy?"

I found him standing with his left fist wrapped like a giant vice around his right wrist. Bright red blood and shiny aluminum paint flowed toward his fingertips mixing together in fancy swirls.

"Daddy! What happened?"

"Paint jar. Broke all to pieces when I tried to open it."

Stunned that he explained it to me without yelling, I stood still with everything open—eyes, mouth, hands. He barked orders as he climbed in the old truck, "You drive!"

I'd never driven the old truck before. I'd never driven anything before. I climbed up, first the running board then the floor board, and then I flopped into the seat in front of the big black steering wheel.

"Put your foot on the clutch." Daddy's calm voice surprised me. "No. The other pedal."

I put my left foot on the small black pad and pushed straightening my leg as far as I could and slid off the seat. Dad, using his left hand yet still holding his wrist, grabbed the knob on the stick shift and pushed it in a back and forth motion.

"Turn the key now."

I did. A noise like ten thousand screeching wolves howled from the engine. And then the shouting, "Push it all the way down!" He took control of the key. The engine roared.

He said, "Push on the gas pedal. Gently."

I wasn't so gentle and the engine raced. "That's enough!" he shouted.

I froze again. He pulled the knob back and said, "Now let out on the clutch. Eaazzzy."

I released, and we jumped forward. The engine died. We tried again and again. Finally, the truck actually moved down the highway on the half-mile trip to grandma's house. After two more gear shifts jumping, shaking, bolting, I turned into the bumpy driveway. Grandpa and mom took over cleaning and purring over the wound.

"It doesn't seem too bad."

"But we can't be too careful, especially since the aluminum paint is in the wound."

"It might be dangerous."

"You never know."

Finally, they decided to take Daddy for stitches.

I found my way to the porch swing with Old Nick, the mongrel dog who loved me like bees love honey, and I sat with him, arms and paws all entwined. We swung gently as I marveled, *I had driven the truck all by myself.*

Truth was, Dad drove through me. I pushed pedals and manned the wheel but Dad directed and corrected and gave me choices. He never let me crash, but I didn't give him the credit. Like I never give God the credit.

Have you felt over-confident and lived as if you didn't need God? Describe how.

Do you long for a more intimate relationship with Jesus? Why?

List several ways you might allow God to lead in your life. What makes you afraid to move forward?

Chapter 17
Victory Party

When discouraged—God is faithful
When defeated—God supernaturally intervenes
When you fear—God sends mercy
When self rises—use God's gifts to seek Him

When you feel your star has gone out and you no longer shine, it is not the end. I have discovered how life can become even brighter than before. Victory over giants is possible. You have talents and abilities. Don't quit before you uncover them. Understanding and utilizing our natural aptitudes and gifts causes us to value life in a new way. But beyond the talents and skills is our God who, because He is faithful, intervenes, sends mercy, and gives gifts. He lights the fire of passion within us.

When I lost my job, I felt the pain deeper than I let on to others and even more than I would let myself believe. Rejection played havoc with my mind. Not only did the company no longer need me, individuals in the office who I considered friends disconnected from me too. I wondered how those people I'd worked with so long were now dealing with all the changes in the office. I speculated whether the quarterly reports showed profit. I thought about my customers and their orders and whether anyone was taking good care of them. And since I'd worked in the grain industry for many years, I longed to know if the annual harvest was plentiful. I'd been consumed by the industry, the company, and the job for more than 30 years, and I couldn't seem to let it go—intellectually or emotionally.

God stepped in. We moved into a wonderful house. It wouldn't be our permanent home but for a time, we were able to live on some acreage with beautiful trees and a constant pleasant breeze. The older house had been newly renovated and had a private swimming pool. There was a place for a garden, and I felt as if I was dancing through life. I converted the guest bedroom into my private morning retreat with a comfortable chair, big windows, and books stacked all around. In those early morning hours, I met God in a new way. I learned how to search for God—not self-fulfillment. As Moses found purpose later in life, I also discovered a new confidence in Him. We began a business. I worked hard, but this time I allowed God to look good. I learned to trust Him for the opportunities to build the business and then gave Him the credit for the successes.

Finding purpose and meaningful work and ministry after a dismal medical diagnosis or a tragedy or a loss isn't easy, but you can do it if you change the focus from self to God.

Belinda led one of the top women's ministries in the country. As a staff member of a large church, she helped women become committed followers of Christ and counseled and comforted those with hurts and struggles. In the middle of these successes, conflicts and disputes and oppositions rose within the church and the tension became unbearable. Eventually, she left the church position, crushed and defeated. In the quiet, painful weeks after leaving, she felt God tug in the direction of a new ministry, clearly understanding God's personal call. The pain of rejection combined with leaving the security of a full-time job, the help of a competent staff, and the prestige of the position required a step into the unknown. With faith and courage, she walked forward.

Following God into the unknown, whether by your choice or by the choice of others (as in my case) is scary and yet the life-interruption can bring much joy—and an exciting new adventure. Our challenge is to trust God completely so that even when our situation is desperate or grueling, we have confidence of the outcome. Author T. W. Hunt called this confidence, "present enjoyment of future blessings." Consider what Hunt's phrase means. We rejoice and delight in our current unfavorable circumstances because we believe God will bring us to the perfect solution filled with blessings and peace.

Trusting God is the challenge. How do we trust Him when our world seems to be falling apart?

Begin with focus on Jesus.

****

My friend Lael was a beauty queen and musician when, at age 29, she was diagnosed with Rheumatoid Arthritis. Now more than 30 years later, though she is often in pain and physically limited by the disease, she is writing books, serving in her church, and helping aspiring writers—and she is one of the world's best encouragers. She is a worldview expert and her presentations inspire audiences across the country to hold to a strong faith in our crippled culture. She hosts beautiful dinners and receptions in her home introducing people to the Lord. When the terrible diagnosis was pronounced, she chose to trust God even though she followed him more out of duty than delight.

Lael says, "For a long time I coped through escape—TV, daydreams. I was living a life divided between God's reality and my own. I sensed the lack of integrity deep in my bones. The reality of my one and only life, full of pain, but also potential moments of love and service to Jesus and others was ticking by. My escapes were killing me softly—one evening of entertainment, one daydream at a time.

"By choosing God, even in the midst of suffering, by getting serious about face time with Jesus, by catching the vision of others who engaged in life as a great conflict where each one is needed, through a renewed vision of our future with Jesus (all woven into my book, *Godsight*), I began to move beyond duty and coping. I began to live from a great desire for God and an outward, kingdom building life, partnering with Jesus in his pursuit of peoples' hearts."

****

My close friend Carole has had more than her share of tragedies. She and her husband faced bankruptcy, and then lost their home in a fire. Then their daughter was standing in the front yard when a drunk driver's car jumped the curb and struck her. After Shari's death, Carole stood in the shower and shook her fist at the devil saying, "Is that all you have? It's not enough to break me. I will trust God." Faith won. But the enemy wasn't finished with Carole. Her mother passed away, and her beloved husband Johnny was diagnosed with stage 4 cancer. Then Hurricane Ike completely destroyed their home and everything in it. She faced it all, trusting the Lord and knowing His sweet love would prevail no matter what problems or tragedies. Carole says,

"I wouldn't trade the deep walk I have with Jesus because of the numerous trials we have gone through. Going through trials drives us deep into His arms for help, strength and comfort. James 1:2-5 says, "Consider it pure joy, my brothers, whenever you face trials of many kinds, because you know that the testing of your faith develops perseverance. Perseverance must finish its work so you may be mature and complete, not lacking anything." Johnny has been in heaven since 2014 but I am exactly where God desires for me to be and I will spend every day that He leaves me here, sharing His love.

****

For believers, tragedy is fuel for greater faith because we know the power and love of God. Read these two verses about the incredible love of God.

"Understand, therefore, that the LORD your God is indeed God. He is the faithful God who keeps his covenant for a thousand generations and lavishes his unfailing love on those who love him and obey his commands" (Deuteronomy 7:9).

"But you, O Lord, are a God of compassion and mercy, slow to get angry and filled with unfailing love and faithfulness" (Psalm 86:15).

God is faithful and loving and never fails to be faithful and loving. Believing Him and trusting that He will work out your tragedies for good is the path to victory.

The Harder Question

As I've faced adversity and loss and tragedy, I have found peace in trusting God, and I've developed a strong faith that He holds my future. I'm grateful for His touch and for the transformation He has made in me—and the giants He has helped me slay.

But the harder question for me is when the giants of discouragement, defeat, fear, and self appear as the direct result of my failure. Can God forgive me for failing? And will He hold my future in His mighty hand when that future is in jeopardy because of my stupidity? And perhaps the hardest question: will He forgive me and work on my behalf when I fail over and over again? Will He step in and crush me? Will He turn His back? What about the pain that I caused?

Do I deserve punishment? The answer is, yes, I do deserve punishment.

But God.

Paul's words express God's heart toward His own,

> "But people are counted as righteous, not because of their work, but because of their faith in God who forgives sinners" (Romans 4:5).

Every sunrise is a new beginning. Every hour. Every minute. I can slay giants because God is gracious and full of mercy. He looks at me and says, "I know. I know." His heart is filled with mercy and forgiveness. He lifts me up and points me to the future He has planned for me.

In the book of Jeremiah, God often spoke against the people of Judah and Jerusalem. He raged against their stubbornness and evil ways. He finally allowed them to go into captivity under Nebuchadnezzar. In captivity, the people cried out, and the Lord said,

> "As soon as Babylon's seventy years are up and not a day before, I'll show up and take care of you as I promised and bring you back home. I know what I'm doing. I have it all planned out—plans to take care of you, not abandon you, plans to give you the future you hope for" (Jeremiah 29:11 The Message).

If we read further in Jeremiah we see how the prophet lived in this hope. He believed God would restore the people (Jeremiah 30:18). He saw the city rebuilt (30:18) and children born (30:20) and the community crops harvested (30:20; 31:4-5). He saw the people go home to find streams of water, level paths, and well-watered gardens. And he declared there would be no more tears as their mourning is turned to gladness. God would be their comfort and joy.

These big promises from God as told by the prophet seemed impossible because of the strength of Babylon.

One morning Jeremiah awoke and realized his sleep had been pleasant. (Jeremiah 31:26). Why? Because he knew God was in control.

He wrote about how much God loved the people,

"They found grace out in the desert,
these people who survived the killing.
Israel, out looking for a place to rest,
met God out looking for them!"
GOD told them, "I've never quit
loving you and never will.
Expect love, love, and more love!
And so now I'll start over with you and build
you up again" (Jeremiah 31:1-4 The Message).

God promised to take the ruins of the nation and make it new (Jeremiah 31:31-32). God always is the author of victory, always the Creator of new life. Always the giant slayer.

If we know God, we know victory. One day you may see that all has finally come together. What you have always wished for has finally come to be. You will look back and laugh at what has passed and you will ask yourself. "How did I get through that!" And like Jeremiah, you may get a good night's sleep.

Perhaps the best example of victory in tragedy is the man Job, whose story is recorded in the Old Testament. Job was wealthy and thriving. He had a large family and everything money could buy. His money did not become a god to him for He faithfully trusted God.

Then tragedy struck. He lost all his wealth and all his family. Fires, vandals, weather, and thieves, and death destroyed all he had built up. Though he vacillated between being overwhelmed and trusting, he had a fire in him that wouldn't quit burning. Though he wished he'd never been born, he believed in God and God's character.

Why did Job suffer?

Job had no idea that a drama about him had played out in heaven. Satan accused that Job's faith was a commercial faith. God accepted the challenge and allowed Satan to bring the disasters to Job. Job was a great and godly man. God knew him; Satan didn't know him.

Job experienced pain. It hurt to see everything and everyone destroyed, and the grief of losing his children was intense. But the reason for his pain was not a test—that's what Satan thought. His trouble was not a punishment—that's what his friends thought. And the moral of his story is not to build patience in us—that's what we've thought for years.

The true reason for Job's pain was to defeat and silence the enemy.

Job was a weapon in the hand of God.

Here's how Job saw his tragedies.

"God alone understands the way to wisdom;
he knows where it can be found,
for he looks throughout the whole earth
and sees everything under the heavens.
He decided how hard the winds should blow

and how much rain should fall.
He made the laws for the rain
and laid out a path for the lightning.
Then he saw wisdom and evaluated it.
He set it in place and examined it thoroughly.
And this is what he says to all humanity:
'The fear of the Lord is true wisdom;
to forsake evil is real understanding'"
(Job 28:23-28).

Job's story proves the worst can be the best if we trust God. His story shows me that if I respond like Job, I'll silence the devil, too.

Use these principles from the Book of Job to live in victory and slay your giants.

- ✛ Every time I trust God, a giant falls.

- ✛ Beware of people who sound like giants telling me what God said or what they saw in a vision about me. *(Speak to God personally and hear Him personally).*

- ✛ Giant talk often *sounds* great. Truth with a mixture of false is false.

- ✛ Giants want me to be so busy defending my theology that I neglect the needs of my friend.

- ✛ Giants rely on logic or reasoning or examples. I will rely on God's Word.

- ✛ Giants lie, saying God is cruel. God is just and God is love. These two opposite characteristics of God are reconciled at the cross.

❖ We have a mediator. His name is Jesus. He is with us as we fight giants.

❖ When you have no answers, cling to your faith.

❖ Beware of giants who claim to know all about God or all about a subject…that claim itself proves they neither know Him nor do they know themselves.

❖ Giants want us to explain God; Giant slayers allow God to reveal himself.

Chapter 18
DVP

I want to be honest about my corporate success. It was great in all the ways I described, but I also felt an emptiness that gnawed at me because often my efforts to become a corporate superstar were not reaping the anticipated rewards. Someone else garnered the bosses' attention. The glass ceiling never fully opened up. A project failed or a deadline passed. When I was successful, showing a profit or increasing sales volume, the bonus check never seemed big enough or came soon enough. I realized that, like Paul, I was absolutely powerless to help myself. (See 2 Corinthians 1:9a TLB). I could do nothing to make my situation better. I was not gratified. I tried. I pushed. I bullied everyone around me. I worked harder than anyone. I took credit for what I did—*and what others did too*. I argued. I won battles. But success never transported me to satisfaction.

DVP

Until I stopped being so proud of myself and my accomplishments. Until I saw God's divine power and provision. Until I understood that I am like a little shepherd boy with a measly slingshot and a few stones. When life looks hopeless from my perspective, it's time to change my point of view, to see through God's eyes, not mine.

> "David said to the Philistine, 'You come against me with sword and spear and javelin, but I come against you in the name of the LORD Almighty'" (1 Samuel 17:45a).

This new sight is divine viewpoint—DVP. Extraordinary, excellent, exceptional lives begin with a new DVP—seeing and thinking in a different way. DVP doesn't compare Goliath to me; DVP juxtaposes Goliath with God. As David said, "for the battle is the LORD's, and he will give all of you into our hands" (1 Samuel 17:47).

Take a good look at the size and power of our God.

> "You, dear children, are from God and have overcome them, because the one who is in you is greater than the one who is in the world" (1 John 4:4-5).

Our problem is that we fix our eyes on the giant but not on God. DVP accepts God's power and promises. He is a giant killer. No longer imprisoned by flat-world thinking or habitual preset notions where false values seem true, we can have reckless confidence in God.

God wants us to see Him as He is. Jesus prayed,

> "Father, I want those you have given me to be with me where I am, and to see my glory, the

glory you have given me because you loved me before the creation of the world" (John 17:24).

The great preacher Jonathan Edwards said, "God desires for us to see His glory—that distinction that makes Him more magnificent and regal than our imaginations can invent. He is higher than the heavens and higher than the angels of heaven. All men, all kings and princes are like worms of the dust before Him. The world's mighty nations are like a drop in a bucket. He rules over the universe and does whatever pleases Him. His knowledge is without bound. His wisdom is perfect and no one can outwit it. His riches are immense and inexhaustible. His majesty is infinitely awesome."[23] And He wants me to know Him in this glorious way. He urges me to see that He is capable of handling any giant that taunts. He invites me to change my perspective to DVP—to see the giant as He sees the giant...beaten.

DVP is possible when we change our horizontal focus to a vertical focus. In Psalm 77, the psalmist described himself as alone, rejected, troubled, unable to sleep, and doubting that God could hear his prayers but then he changed his focus from himself to God. He considered the deeds, miracles, and works of God.

"Your ways O God are holy. What god is so great as our God?" (Psalm 77:13).

He made faith's decision to look beyond the present troubles and God's bewildering inactivity, to draw hope anew from God's greatness.[24] By shifting the focus to God's glory, he found hope and peace.

When our focus changes to a DVP, we march out to the valley floor carrying our homemade slingshot as if it were the world's greatest weapon. With DVP, we see the faithfulness of God clearly, and we lean into the mercy of God and count on

His intervening hand. In the hands of God, we have confidence, hope, and peace. Jesus said,

> "I have told you these things, so that in me you may have peace. In this world you will have trouble. But take heart! I have overcome the world" (John 16:33).

He has overcome the world and all the giants!

****

Jesus saw with DVP when Judas betrayed him. "Jesus, knowing all that was going to happen to him, went out and asked them, 'Who is it you want?'" (John 18:4). Though He could foresee the beatings, the abuse, and the pain, He faced His tormentors boldly. In God's plan, He was safe while they cracked the flogging whip. Jesus answered,

> "You would have no power over me if it were not given to you from above" (John 19:11).

Paul saw with DVP when

> "Some Jews came from Antioch and Iconium and won the crowd over. They stoned Paul and dragged him outside the city, thinking he was dead. But after the disciples had gathered around him, he got up and went back into the city" (Acts 14:19-21).

They stoned him, rejected his message, nearly killed him, yet Paul went right back into the battle to face the pious, religious, arrogant giant. His purpose was to spread the gospel, and he could see God's protection even in opposition.

Isaiah understood DVP.

"Though the mountains be shaken and the hills be removed, yet my unfailing love for you will not be shaken nor my covenant of peace be removed," says the LORD, who has compassion on you" (Isaiah 54:10).

****

Our whole world could fall apart—job disintegrate, finances down the tube, relationships fizzle, pain, illness, death, mountains shaking and falling—yet God still loves us and has compassion on us. Grasp the enormity of Isaiah's principle. God, the same one who created all things and keeps the world operating, has compassion on you when the giant challenges you. See Him in His glory, and you'll see your giant from His eyes.

DVP.

Remember in chapter 1, when Paul said he was doomed to die, but that was *good*. With DVP I see how doomed I am. I know I can't help myself. But that is good! Because then, and only then, can I trust God. You may be wondering how you can trust God enough to go into the valley to face your giant. You may be thinking. I want to but I am too frightened.

He knows how frightened you are. He knew you would be coming to this day. He is not surprised that you are here at the end of your rope. He knew you would need some strength to make this choice. That's why he showed himself to you last year or years ago in that small way. That's why he stirred your heart when you read your Bible last week or as you've read about these four giants. So that you would have courage when the giant screams. David was keeping sheep. He had one job—keep those sheep safe. When a bear came, he overcame it with God's help. When the lion came, he hit his mark with his slingshot. God was there. Then he faced the biggest human anyone had ever seen, but he remembered that God was with him. He took a step out on to the valley floor.

With DVP, we are no longer hostages to our bad choices. Like the woman at the well, our lives are not instantly changed, but our choice to see from God's point of view alters the future. In his book, *Messy Spirituality*, Author Michael Yaconelli explained, "We don't have to wait until we are mature. We don't have to move to a new town or convince others that we are serious; we simply start. We begin. We take the first bumbling, stumbling, teetering steps...."[25]

Without DVP, we walk around with an inner dullness. Author Mark Buchanan calls it "spiritual sleepwalking, a kind of chronic stuckness. We learn much about God and at the same time we grow distant from God; we will study the intricacies of doctrine, but lose passion; we will become eloquent in God talk, but cease talking to God."[26]

Lee Strobel, author of *The Case for Christ*, said that faith is taking a step in the same direction that the evidence is pointing. David's evidence pointed in the direction of the giant. He remembered the bear and the lion, and he believed. He took the step in that direction, and God met him.

Moses said much the same thing when he remembered Israel's battles.

> "The LORD your God, who is going before you,
> will fight for you, as he did for you in Egypt,
> before your very eyes, and in the desert.
> There you saw how the LORD your God carried
> you, as a father carries his son, all the way you
> went until you reached this place"
> (Deuteronomy 1:30-31 NIV).

He fought for you back in Egypt, and He will go before you to fight for you again. In fact, He will carry you like a father carries his son.

How do we gain divine perspective? Though we don't face Goliaths every day, we face smaller obstacles. When we overcome the smaller giants, we build the courage and perspective we need to face Goliath and his brothers.

Trusting God, and allowing Him to speak instead of me, became a stepping stone of evidence that I could trust Him. He helped me build better instincts and discernment so that I made wiser decisions in the future. How different some situations would have ended if I have begun trusting God for daily decisions. At the end of me and my professional prowess, God stepped in.

Small battles won week after week in attitude and in substance are the battles that make me strong enough to trust God to go into the valley and face the giant.

Choose to Fight Your Giant

You can choose today to cower behind the tent as Saul and his men did, or you can step out carrying whatever strengths and weaknesses you own, grabbing whatever tools you have, defeating the giant with faith in Jesus Christ.

Every person who never killed a giant will tell you it's impossible. But the giants represent more than we can see. God may allow your giant battles so that you will grow spiritually and mentally. God may allow the enemy to send a giant to you so you can be a weapon against Satan. Coming face to face with your giant is not an accident. It's a divine appointment. God knows where you are.

After the Battles

After spending more than 30 years in the corporate world, fighting the turf battles and pushing against that glass ceiling, I was in the beige house. I'd never spent much time alone at home before. I missed the excitement and thrill of crafting, proposing, and following through on projects, business deals, and big sales. I missed seeing people every day. I missed dressing up. I missed my big private office. I was also deeply hurt with the pain of loss and angered at the injustice of being downsized out of my job. No one from the office called to see how I was doing. No one cared that I was alone. I realized I had few real friends there.

I couldn't get a grip on what my new life would be and the beige house didn't help. My grandchildren were nearby, and I loved being with those funny and interesting little personalities. I tried to organize our home and cook and go out into the new surroundings. But deep inside my feelings were sad and empty.

One day I received a phone call from our state's Institute of Transportation. *Who knew we had one!* Someone had given them my name and suggested I would be a good editor for reports they were publishing. I worked for them, which meant they sent reports digitally, and I edited them on the computer in my home, in my p.j.s on my time schedule. We welcomed the money but performing significant work fueled my recovery.

Someone had given them my name?

I learned that the person who gave them my name was a friend whom I had not seen or talked to for more than 10 years. Why did she think of me? How did she connect to the Institute? Coincidence?

No. God orchestrated the events so that at the moment they needed an editor and I needed to feel productive and useful, God intervened.

In the next few years, other opportunities came my way, always to work at home and always growing me as a person and as a professional. I worked for non-profits and businesses and individuals. Each job took me to a new level of proficiency and expertise. I attended seminars and conferences and received coaching in speaking and writing from some of the nation's top coaches. Each year brought new challenges and exciting breaks. One year I helped several different authors develop books—using my skills as an editor, writer, and coach and learning new skills in the world of book production. These authors had valid reasons for self-publishing their book. One was a psychologist and teacher who was sending Xeroxed copies of his materials to groups using his curriculum. Publishing a book gave him a more professional vehicle for those materials. Another was a woman who had developed a wonderful ministry for those facing infertility. Her published book had a ready audience in all the groups which were springing up in churches around the country. One woman was a brilliant Bible teacher in a large church and people wanted to buy her book. *(In the Appendix, I have written my thoughts on traditional publishing and self-publishing and what you should consider if you want to write and publish a book.)*

In January of that next year, I took a week-long sabbatical with some friends at a lovely retreat center. One of those friends was author, speaker Carol Kent. She asked me what I had been doing, and I told her about the authors and the books. The next day she said, "I think you should start thinking of the name of your publishing imprint and start a new publishing company."

The idea seemed far-fetched, and I laughed, but her voice seemed to be the voice of God speaking into my life. I returned home and told George. And we laughed. *Of course, that makes sense*, we thought. *We have no experience, no employees, no equipment, no warehouse, no expertise, no money....* So, we began a publishing company—Bold Vision Books.

The journey has been full of highs and lows and excitement and panic—and hard work. From the beginning, we have wanted the business to be service and ministry more than about money.

The reason I tell you those details is because I want you to know how giant killing has played a role in the operation of the company and in our lives.

I could describe hundreds of situations, some of them related to authors and books but many related to finances, in the years since we began BVB. Each one brought the giants of discouragement, defeat, fear, and self. *We don't have enough money to pay the bills or to start this project or to travel to a place. I don't know how to help this author because of personality differences or misunderstandings or lack of time.*

I tend to go to the lowest point and wonder what we will do. Then God shows up. Someone buys a quantity of books. A client pays an invoice. A new coaching or editing job comes along. A bid is accepted.

Because God is faithful and He intervenes with mercy and grace.

God is also faithful when I feel overwhelmed by the volume of work. He reminds me how he made each person with different personalities, skills, assets, and yes, flaws. Sometimes when I'm at my wit's end with a person's behavior or lack of progress, a verse in my daily devotion will remind me to be kind, merciful, and humble.

I am grateful for His faithfulness. I depend on it and my trust in Him is valid because He always shows up; He is always faithful.

And when I hit bottom and defeat overwhelms, He is still there helping me kill the giant. Once, it seemed I couldn't finish an edit job. The more I worked the more the job seemed never ending. Every paragraph took longer than it should take. Every page was filled with problems that needed too much explanation or so many changes that I became the writer not the editor. My discouragement slid right down the slope into defeat. I did what I'm sometimes best suited for—I panicked. I felt the only choice was to quit—send the manuscript and the pre-payment back to the author and then take down the website and close the company. *Yes, I still go there—and it is the darkest place.*

Then God intervenes.

In the case of the never-ending editing job, the deadline was extended. Really? God can do the impossible. In the case of the difficult client, an email arrives telling me how happy and thrilled the client is to be working with me. Yes, really.

When we feel defeated, God intervenes and entwines himself into our situation.

The giants of fear and self show up regularly too. God is faithful, involved, and merciful, and He provides all I need to win each battle.

In those days when I was so self-confident and proud of all I could do, I would never have dreamed that I would become so dependent on Him.

Give a girl a giant…and she fights for her life.

Epilogue

The old man rose slowly from the low couch. He rubbed his knees, feeling the pain of too many battles, too many nights in wilderness camps with his mighty men.

Flashbacks of clashes with brutal barbarians, sounds of thundering horses, and a lingering memory of the giant flood his mind. He looked out to the golden city of Jerusalem, now peaceful. Yesterday he had joined the worshiping throngs on the mount where his son would build the temple of God.

Grief sent its sharp spikes into his heart reminding how he'd failed with his other children. *O Absalom.* Memories sped through his mind. He had sinned against God Almighty in the most egregious ways, but God knew his inmost heart, which was mostly quick to repent. In discouraging times, his faithlessness always found God's faithfulness. When defeat had roared, God dipped his fingers into the matters of mortals and intervened. And when the old man's greatest fears had overwhelmed, God was merciful. But the greatest lesson of all had been putting selfish desires away and following the will of God using God's gifts. A song came to mind; he hummed the tune and mumbled the words,

"The LORD is my light and my salvation—
so why should I be afraid? The LORD is my
fortress, protecting me from danger, so why
should I tremble?" (Psalm 27:1).

God had been his strength and power from the beginning when he was a boy shepherding the sheep and through his long life when he battled enemies without and within. Now he turned his head upward and prayed for the future.

"How great you are, O Sovereign LORD! There
is no one like you. We have never even heard
of another God like you! What other nation
on earth is like your people Israel? What other
nation, O God, have you redeemed from slavery
to be your own people? You made a great name
for yourself when you redeemed your people
from Egypt. You performed awesome miracles
and drove out the nations and gods that
stood in their way. You made Israel your
very own people forever, and you, O
LORD, became their God.

"And now, O LORD God, I am your servant; do
as you have promised concerning me and my
family. Confirm it as a promise that will last
forever. And may your name be honored forever
so that everyone will say, 'The LORD of Heaven's
Armies is God over Israel!' And may the house
of your servant David continue before you
forever" (2 Samuel 7:22-26).

The room felt cold and damp. He shivered.

"Then David died and was buried with his ancestors in the City of David. David had reigned over Israel for forty years, seven of them in Hebron and thirty-three in Jerusalem. Solomon became king and sat on the throne of David his father, and his kingdom was firmly established" (1 Kings 2:10-12).

"The Lord is near to all who call on Him, to all who call on Him in truth. He fulfills the desire of those who fear Him; he also hears their cry and saves them" (Psalm 145:18-19).

Acknowledgments

Thank you George for your never ending encouragement. Thank you to my children, Cherry, Craig, Brett, and Kathryn. Thank you to the greatest grands, Ashton, Garrett, Gracen, Clayton, and Gabi. You light up my life.

Thank you Carole Lewis. You are my everyday encourager. I treasure your friendship.

Thank you to my agent, Janet Grant of Books and Such Literary Agency. So glad to call you friend.

To my weekly FP sisters who inspire me with your grace and faith: Pam Farrell, Grace Fox, Lauraine Snelling, Becky Turner, Carole Lewis, Cynthia Ruchti, Vicki Heath, Mary Ward, Wendy Lawton, Cindy McDowell, and Carol Kent.

Thank you Rhonda Rhea for saying I could do it. You energize me.

About the Author

 **Karen Porter** is an international speaker, a successful business woman, and the author or co-author of seven books (including *Speak Like Jesus* and *I'll Bring the Chocolate)*. She writes for *Leading Hearts* magazines and is a *Guideposts* author.

She is president of Advanced Writers and Speakers Association, and president of the First Place 4 Health board of directors and serves on several other national boards. Karen coaches aspiring writers and speakers. She and her husband George own Bold Vision Books a Christian publishing company.

Karen says her greatest achievement is her marriage to George. In her spare time, she follows her lifelong quest to find the perfect purse.

Connect with Karen at www.karenporter.com

Look for Karen's regular leadership column in *Leading Hearts* Magazine.

Appendix

A note about self-publishing. I don't often recommend self-publishing unless the author has a valid and compelling reason for going the self-published route. Some of those reasons might be the following.

The author already has a following or audience who will purchase the book. For example, a teacher of a large group, a person who has built a curriculum or program as an outlet; a pastor or leader in a large church or denomination who has a ready audience.

The author has written a book that is specific for a limited group. For example, a family history that would only be purchased by members of that family or a niche book that targets a small segment of people interested in that topic.

With digital printing companies popping up everywhere, it is tempting and easy to self-publish. But before you do, understand the pros and cons. If you choose to go the self-published route, don't go down that road alone. Get advice. Find an editor—one who will not only make all the punctuation and grammar correct but one who will help you develop the content and challenge you to write your best. Pay an artist to design a custom cover. Get help from a professional to print and distribute the book. Beware of those who over-charge for self-publishing and provide minimum editing, use bland template designs, and then charge you extra for costly, and often ineffective, marketing.

Endnotes

[1] The Philistines were defiant warriors who had developed sophisticated weapons of iron. Known as "sea people," the Philistines came from Indo-Europe and Crete and established city-states on the Mediterranean Coast and inland at Gaza, Askelon, Ekron, and Gath. Webster's Dictionary gives one of the primary definitions of "Philistine" as a metaphor for "brutish and boorish warrior," and biblical history shows how these strong and vicious fighters conquered the land. Modern archaeologists have excavated many of these Palestine's city-states and found a sophisticated culture with structure, industry, and art. One of their claims to fame is the brewing of beer and making of wine. Archaeologists have unearthed complex breweries and beer mugs from these sites. Some skeptical intellectuals have touted in the New York Times and elsewhere that these discoveries prove the Bible is wrong because these classy, refined Philistines couldn't have been the vicious warriors that are depicted. But why does one have to make the other untrue? I see no conflict that brutal warriors could enjoy the arts and entertainment and behave well when not on the battlefield. And anyone who ever dealt with an alcoholic knows how a person's behavior changes and declines when they are drunk. Read the story of Samson in Judges 14-16 and see how rowdy and perverse the crowd becomes as the party gets wilder.

Archaeological finds are wonderful and useful, but they are not complete. We don't know what else the digs will tell, so no one can definitely say that the Philistines were a nice, kind, gentle people or that the Bible is false with these few finds in the digs.

Read the story of Samson again and consider how they gouged out his eyes. Read about the other battles to see how brutal and vicious and frightening these warriors were.

2 https://billygraham.org/story/billy-graham-answers-commonly-asked-questions-about-easter/

3 A foreign conglomerate had purchased our company and eventually eliminated all the US management personnel. I was among the first to go.

4 C.S. Lewis, *The Screwtape Letters*, Harper One; Reprint Edition, 2015, p. 7

5 *International Bible Encyclopedia*

6 Thank you to my pastor, Garrett Booth, Senior Pastor Grace Church, Houston for this life-changing quote.

7 T. W. Hunt, *Mind of Christ*, B&H Books, 1997

8 Read Philippians 4 to see how He humbled himself from the glory of heaven to the status of a human living on the flawed earth.

9 https://science.howstuffworks.com/life/inside-the-mind/emotions/fear.htm

10 Some translations say the name of this giant is Goliath. Most scholars agree that a better translation is "brother of Goliath." According to 1 Chronicles 20:5 the name of this giant is Lahmi.

11 http://www.emotionalcompetency.com/fear.htm

12 https://www.psychologytoday.com/us/blog/intimacy-path-toward-spirituality/201404/deconstructing-the-fear-rejection

13 https://www.psychologytoday.com/us/basics/fear

14 Denis Wailey

15 Dictionary.com/browse/mercy

16 https://www.desiringgod.org/articles/have-mercy-on-me

17 Jennifer Kennedy Dean, *Altar'd: Experience the Power of Resurrection*, New Hope Publishers, 2012

18 https://www.nytimes.com/roomfordebate/2016/10/06/should-every-young-athlete-get-a-trophy/participation-trophies-send-a-dangerous-message

19 Oswald Chambers, *My Utmost for His Highest*, Feb 12, https://utmost.org/are-you-listening-to-god/

20 https://www.allaboutgod.com/listening-to-god.htm

[21] C. S. Lewis, *Mere Christianity*, Touchstone, New York, 1996. P 190.

[22] C. S. Lewis

[23] "The Excellency of Christ," Jonathan Edwards, Sermon, August 1736

[24] NIV Study Bible Notes, Ps 77:10-12

[25] Michael Yaconelli, *Messy Spirituality*, Zondervan, 2002, page 65

[26] Mark Buchanan, *Your God is Too Safe*, Multnomah Publishers, Inc., 2001, page 21

Other Books by Karen Porter

I'll Bring the Chocolate

A fun and rich book comparing all the luscious qualities of chocolate to all the luscious qualities of women's friendships.

Speak Like Jesus

Straight from Karen's coaching for speakers, readers will learn the art of presentation.

Invite Karen Porter to your event. She will bring laughter, fun, and joy.

But laughter is only the beginning.

www.karenporter.com